# UNLOCKING LEADERSHIP

# UNLOCKING LEADERSHIP

## *The* SCHOOL PERSPECTIVE

**SEEMA MALIK**

FOREWORD BY DR NARENDRA JADHAV

Konark Publishers Pvt Ltd
New Delhi · Seattle

**Konark Publishers Pvt. Ltd**
206, First Floor,
Peacock Lane, Shahpur Jat,
New Delhi 110 049
Phone: +91-11-41055065
e-mail: india@konarkpublishers.com
website: www.konarkpublishers.com

**Konark Publishers International**
8615, 13th Ave SW,
Seattle WA 98106
Phone: (415) 409-9988
e-mail: us@konarkpublishers.com



ISBN: 978-81-949286-7-6

Edited by Dipali Singh

Cover Design by Misha Oberoi

Cover image ©Shutterstock

Typeset by Saanvi Graphics, Noida

Printed and bound at Thomson Press (India) Ltd

*My first book is dedicated to*
*the Takshila Educational Society,*
*which gave me the wings of opportunities*
*to grow and achieve my goals*

# Contents

# FOREWORD

## Vision and Practice of Educational Leadership

This book, written by a practicing school principal, delves into various school leadership styles. The author's vast experience of leading schools across different geographies and cultures of the country has made this anecdote-rich and research-driven book very thought-provoking.

What principals do for making a difference in the organization—by leading change, promoting organizational learning at each level and influencing systems and processes to have desired outcomes—has long captured the attention of educationists globally. It is unequivocally accepted that the quality of leadership makes a significant difference to school and student outcomes. Although, there is a rich body of literature and research in the western world pertaining to school leadership, this does not seem to have happened in India, as yet. As the country's economy gathers pace and gets more connected globally, schools also recognize that building human resource is a prerequisite for staying competitive; and today, dynamism requires not only trained and committed teachers but also highly effective principals.

It is the school leadership that directs and guides the way schools are run through policies and systems, the way teachers work for the upliftment and improvement of education and the manner in which students achieve their learning outcomes. Coordinated relationships, teamwork, motivation and the entire school culture revolve around the vision of the school leader. The ultimate goal of a school leader is to make the school effective through organisational efficiency, teachers' job satisfaction, students' engagement with learning and the community's participation in the school ecosystem. It goes without saying that the role of a school leader is transformational.

While the need for effective leaders is acknowledged, there is much less agreement on what leadership style is more likely to produce favourable outcomes. There are numerous models of leadership, each with its own distinctive approach and influence on the followers. Managerial style of leading schools is focused on managing existing activities successfully rather than envisioning a better future for the organisation. A school principal is not just a 'policy implementer', he/she carries a moral imperative too. Transformational leaders with higher levels of personal commitment to organisational goals influence and raise the level of moral qualms, resulting in the goals of leaders and followers coalescing into a genuine and harmonious relationship. There are also Participative leaders who succeed in bonding the staff together, Collaborative leaders who share responsibilities with team members to build more leaders for future, and also Transactional leaders who believe in building relationships based on exchange for resources. There are also leaders who model their behaviour and engage with all stakeholders through dialogue and discussion. They nurture ideas, identify issues, resolve tensions, enable systems and empower stakeholders.

This book cohesively intertwines the experience of the author as a school leader in Indian schools for the past two decades with the theory and practices learnt through her formal education in school leadership at Cambridge University. The author's motivation for writing this book has emanated from her more than 20 years of experience in leading schools across India. Its 16 chapters focus on research-grounded findings to build upon the leadership knowledge that different school leaders possess naturally. The book has an international perspective as well as a national frame of reference.

The book attempts to describe different leadership models in the world of education—each one of them having its own salient features, merits as well as weaknesses. It illustrates how principals lead through delegation, partnering, collaboration and innovation to shape the ethos of the school. This research work with compelling real-life accounts explores how to influence the lives of students and teachers. It will give new insights into the policy and practice of educational leadership. Every school leader will be able to relate to these leadership models and place themselves at a vantage point.

I wish the book a grand success.

New Delhi **Dr Narendra Jadhav**
30 August 2021

# Acknowledgements

Deepest thanks to my children—Mugdha and Kshitij—who believed in me, and my mother who stood by me through thick and thin while I worked in deep reverie every evening. They all encouraged me to write.

I am indebted to Takshila Educational Society, for this book would not have been possible without their unwavering support and financial assistance. I wish to express my sincere appreciation to Mr Sanjiv Kumar, who is an educational leader par excellence and a living example of motion leadership.

Dr Narendra Jadhav, the intellectual who wears numerous hats as a public policy expert, a noted economist, educationist, professor and writer, inspired me to write this book. Serendipitously, I came to know him during a webinar hosted for NEP 2020 and from there began my dream of writing a book which was in the pipeline for a decade but materialized only after meeting with him. My heartfelt thanks to him for writing the Foreword for this book.

The three decades of working with many school leaders and colleagues have helped me pen down my experiences in the form of this book. All of them cannot be named here but their contributions will always be valuable. My last school experience guided me further when in just a single organization, I met and worked with at least 10 different types of school leaders, each with their own strength and style.

The numerous teachers I worked with brought to life the research and reflection of over a decade of teaching and leading. They were highly motivating and intrinsically driven to give life to my vision for the school. All the leadership theories could be seen being played out day in, day out in this laboratory of life.

Professor Peter Gronn, my PhD guide, shaped my writing during the years I spent studying in Cambridge University.

Last but not the least, special thanks to my publisher Mr K.P.R. Nair and his team at Konark Publishers who helped in shaping my manuscript into the book you are reading now.

# INTRODUCTION
## Changing Metaphors of Leadership

Over the last several decades, a rich theoretical and empirical body of literature has tried to understand the contribution of leadership in school performance. Leadership acts as a catalyst without which positive progress is quite unlikely to happen. The study of educational leadership has gained a lot of prominence in the last three decades. All interventions regarding school reforms emanate from the school leader's office. Yet, the concept of leadership remains as elusive as ever. A search for any commonly accepted leadership style is futile but it would be worthwhile to know what the possibilities and opportunities of school leadership are. Many scholars distinguish management from leadership with research evidence and common perception. Managerial activities should aim to efficiently and effectively shape the organizational arrangements, focusing on maintenance. These activities are designed to produce stability. Leadership, on the other hand, involves influencing others to achieve existing or new goals, transforming existing ways and promoting change.

The 'managerial imperative' often dominates the work of school leaders. Indeed, successful school leadership can even transform the entire community around it and through it, the larger society. Undoubtedly, the efforts to change and preserve are often blended in the practice of leaders as multitaskers. For example, maintaining scheduling arrangements for teachers that create opportunities for them to meet with one another can enable instructional innovation. Leaders who neglect managerial concerns may have difficulties in leading change. Further, while the management versus leadership distinction is helpful as a theoretical tool, in practice, there is nothing like 'purely management' and 'purely leadership' per se.

An in-depth analysis of school leadership merits attention in India since greater emphasis has been placed in academic writing on political, industry and social leaders. However, school leaders are akin to social leaders since they can bring a lot of change in how the society thinks through its children, who in turn get influenced by the school culture. The appointment and retention of a new principal is emerging from research evidence as one of the most important strategies for turning around schools.

Having been a school leader for almost two decades in leading private schools of India, I came across a number of school leaders, all with different styles of leading. Some were more managerial in style and others charismatic, just as some were transactional with formal authority vested in them and others, transformational with a long-term vision for their organization. Every time I looked at a situation,

I thought about whether there was a school vision. Was it being articulated well by the principal? Was there a strategic plan to achieve it? All leaders were unique in their way of addressing these questions.

Each to their own! They all succeeded in their own way and there was never any one typical style to delimit and define the ideal school leadership. As a young teacher at the beginning of my career, I worked with school leaders who were clearly authoritarian in their style, with, for example, pin-drop silence in the school as the USP of their competence. Over a period of time, I also worked under leaders who were so democratic, bordering at the laissez-faire style, that teachers working under them lost a clear direction for which they had to strive.

A few years further down the line, I worked under a school leader who believed in creating autonomous teams which could take their own decisions, keeping in mind the larger good of the school. While there was a formal principal and a vice principal, there was also a number of group leaders to whom leadership tasks were delegated. The team members worked under the team leader but were free to voice their opinions, which were invariably heard and taken notice of. The most successful school leaders were open-minded and ready to learn from others. They were also flexible rather than dogmatic in their thinking within the system of core values, persistent, resilient and optimistic. Such traits help explain why successful leaders facing daunting challenges are often able to push forward when there is little reason to expect progress.

After heading schools for more than two decades, I thought of penning my thoughts about school leadership. I developed a new perspective after having lived and studied at Cambridge University, UK. There was a stark contrast to what I had experienced in India, not only owing to the cultural differences but also due to the necessity of undergoing leadership training before taking over the helm of an organization new to me.

Research-based findings and evidence gave a solid grounding to the training in school leadership. There were deputy leaders (vice principals) and senior teachers who were heavily into instructional leadership with hands-on experience of classroom transactions with teachers and sat through curriculum discussions, working for assessment plans. No wonder then, that the nomenclature also varied for them—they were 'head teachers' in letter and spirit. As a typical principal, a 'head teacher' was not the first among equals but one among equals, enjoying greater support of his/her followers.

To me, who had till then only had the experience of Indian schooling, it opened a whole new world to my understanding of school leadership. While sitting in the lecture hall with many class fellows, there were many things which came to me as an utter surprise. Some of them were already the head teachers of various schools while some were preparing for the coveted role with the course that we were all undergoing in school leadership. These head teachers would often be found immersed in some lesson plans, correcting them, writing their remarks and discussing them with the others, as if they were the ones who were going to teach in the classroom. It was all so new to me since most principals I knew were larger than life and their expected role was to guide and mentor everybody from a high pedestal. The in-depth discussion on pedagogy and theories of learning was a rare, if not an impossible, aspect of school principalship.

After four years spent researching in Cambridge University, I thought of sharing my insights with people I worked with. Leadership is no longer an on-the-job training but a phenomenon grounded in real research in schools. Decades of research has already revealed that collaboration and collegiality are essential qualities of school leadership, that the best of intentions go awry when they are not accepted willingly by the teachers. This happens particularly when the school system is highly centralized. Of course, there can be contrived collegiality that could be administratively controlled, compulsory and non-negotiable, but it might not have the wherewithal to lead to meaningful and sustainable changes.

While engaging with so many class-fellows in a joyous banter, much after the study hours, it was a fresh change of perspective about leadership. They knew each teacher's family background, strengths and weaknesses, way of teaching and even visited them at home in times of any challenge they faced. Clearly, they seemed like one of the teachers with many more in the school, albeit with a formal position and authority. 'Head Teachers' in letter and spirit!

As a school leader, I have often found that sharing and analysing information with teachers improved student achievement and parent satisfaction. Data alone doesn't make decisions, people do! The teacher's own knowledge, experience and intuition are important ingredients in school decisions. The single most important factor affecting school improvement is the leadership, a fact that goes without saying. The questions to be asked are:

- Is the leader able to drive teachers towards the common purpose and vision of the school?
- Can the leader carry the whole team forward towards excellence?
- Does the morale of teachers remain high in spite of any real or perceived setback?
- Do teachers have enough confidence in the school leader for steering them professionally to reach a higher level of achievement?

At the heart of school capacity is the principal, focused on the development of teachers' knowledge and skills development, professional community, programme coherence and motivation for achieving the school goals. Schools need to adapt to the changing environments for which we need leaders who can guide and motivate the students and teachers to evolve intellectually, socially and emotionally—in a continuous process. Successful leaders view their organization's environment in a holistic way by not only deepening their own understanding of the organizational culture but also challenging their own view on leadership. This helps them to shape their values, beliefs, attitudes and expectations for promoting a stable and nurturing learning environment. Principals who are able to adapt their vision to new changes and the development of the environment will be able to build strong schools. The popular distinction between 'doing things right' for management and 'doing right things' for leadership is not really a cookie-cutter difference. It's time we changed the metaphors for leadership.

# 1

# Leaders Demonstrate What is Possible

In the 1990s, across the world, the term 'Instructional Leadership' became very popular. The rising focus on instructional leadership in India came as public schools brought in more accountability in the areas of student performance, teachers' training, their performance appraisal and the clear acknowledgement that the leadership of principals is finally the door at which the buck stops. With this accountability movement, the actions of principals gained more currency in the school administration. It was no longer about the perfunctory role of the principal as a figurehead but about the newer concept of leadership density. These principals could turn the school around with their direct interest and intervention. Clearly, strong and direct leadership focused on the curriculum gives the principal not only expertise, but also confers charisma. Such principals are always hands-on, digging deep into the real

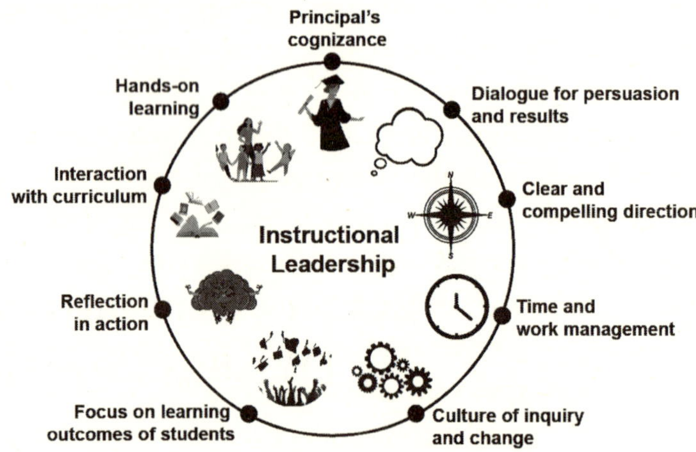


**Fig.1: Instructional Leadership**

classroom curriculum and interaction, and happy to work with teachers. They are culture builders for the school with a very direct focus only on the curriculum transaction. Instructional leaders are effective communicators and since they are not office-bound armchair principals, their presence is very visible in the school (Fig. 1). However, their eloquence is not just slogan raising but gets disseminated with the best results.

For teachers to meet the challenges of the emerging schools' expectations, they need to depend more on what they learn in practice rather than what they learnt while studying. This 'reflection in action' comes seamlessly from instructional leaders. It is a known but sad fact of many schools that they keep running in auto modes, believing firmly that what they have been doing for years can go on for many more years to come. To empower teachers with the practice of reflection, deeply involved instructional principals can play a major role in processes like inquiry, thinking and assessing, exploration and experimentation in schools.

As a newly trained senior geography teacher in one of the leading private schools in Delhi, I found myself interacting on a daily basis with the vice principal of the school who was a geography teacher par excellence. Each one of my free periods during the day was spent in observing his classes which initially seemed like drudgery with the enormous workload I had besides reading and preparing for lessons. However, in no time I started looking forward to his classes. In spite of the fact that he was the deputy leader of a large school, with long hours put in every day, the enthusiasm that he generated was highly infectious.

As I started sitting through his classes, it became clear to me why it was so. Suddenly I found myself challenging my own assumptions about teaching the subject in which I had continually excelled through school and university. What the best of Bachelor of Education (BEd) colleges couldn't teach their students, I was learning in his class. He made even the most technical topics very interesting, transporting his listeners to the landscape or geographical feature that he was talking about. The diagrams and maps he used were sheer art on the board and his voice modulation absolutely delightful. It was through laughter and fun that not only students learnt but so did the teachers who observed him. That, to me, was an excellent example of instructional leadership which I experienced myself, much before I came across this term.

Teachers find such leaders working with them, sitting through their lessons and giving feedback to them directly. They turn the school mission into transferable student learning outcomes. They set high standards for teachers as well as students, managing the instructional programme on their own. The entire school is visibly enthused with their learning focus. Teachers know that they have clear and measurable goals which have to be achieved for the continuous academic progress of the school. The leader or principal takes the responsibility to ensure that the goals are not only clearly known to everyone but so are the strategies outlined to realize their achievement. The academic mission is communicated to the staff at every opportunity. With an ongoing dialogue with the teachers, many aspects of the methodology for teaching with learning outcomes get discussed.

Innovative teachers seek out such instructional leaders to be heard and to get encouragement, while those who face classroom challenges meet such principals for counsel and advice. Such principals are friendly yet firm when conveying what ought to be done for the school. They delineate the role expectations to teachers articulately and when required, play the peacemaker in any conflict between them. Such principals, by their own behaviour and demeanour, set the role expectations. Aided with observation, common sense and intuition, they run a well-steered ship sailing through all weathers. They are comfortable in consulting with the teachers when required—and even when not required—to get the team on their side.

Besides managing the instructional programme, such leaders focus on coördination and control of instruction. They supervise and evaluate instruction, coordinate the curriculum and relentlessly monitor student progress. Such principals play managerial, human resource and professional development roles for their schools. They keep adjusting to the opportunities and constraints the school context imposes on them, which is very important in how they set the stage for the optimum performance. As new understandings keep evolving about school progress, they keep moulding their leadership. Some of the elements of the school context are student backgrounds, the larger community within which the school operates, resources available to the school, organizational structure, teachers' experience and their competence. Since instructional leadership is a mutual process of the principal and the teacher influencing each other, principals keep responding to the changing context.

It goes without saying that the most difficult job of an instructional leader is to change the existing culture of the school for the better. A common refrain of teachers is the stubborn 'this is the way we do things here', showing the resistance to change. I, too, have been the direct recipient of such comments. In a school where systems and processes were unheard of, every action depended on the whims and fancies of the school authorities. Since there was no protocol for getting things done by a set process, developing a method of functioning that dealt with each case in a unique way, often bordering on the laissez-faire policy, caused heartburn among teachers and parents. When I began this way of functioning, I initiated motivating teachers to try out a better alternative without making them feel threatened. It was a slow process but by virtue of hand-holding the teachers over a few months, success came sooner than later. Surprisingly, the teachers themselves became the ambassadors of this change, once they bought into the vision and mission of the school leader.

Within days of my joining the school as principal, the personal assistant to the principal who had been working there for more than two decades, came with a file containing printouts of many emails. She requested me to write the replies to those emails so that she could send them. Not only was I stupefied but also appalled that she had access to all my emails and was taking their prints, wasting precious paper. I sat her down and asked her how she could access these emails when they were clearly addressed to me. At this, she told me that she has been doing it forever and she assumed the practice would continue. I asked her to stop doing that and then changed the password. When I told her that I would access the emails myself and write to the senders, she was pleasantly amused and asked me what would her work be then! From there, however, responsibilities were delineated for her and it became a water-cooler discussion point in the school. Gradually, teachers and the administrative staff got used to this so-called 'new development'.

Similarly, giving undue and out-of-turn increments to teachers was also the way of functioning of the school chairman, which brought in a lot of discrimination among teachers. Sycophancy was the criterion for promotions and that led to many undeserving candidates getting better positions. Opportunities for foreign jaunts were given to his sycophants on all-expenses-paid basis. It was also common for some teachers to get away with any lapses with the help of their special positions conferred on them by the principal who had a close coterie of confidants. However, as the system started taking root for procedures and policies with transparency, everyone discovered the strength of performance-based increments and promotions, which weren't based on *who brought what gifts and goodies for the principal* but *who performed better than the others* for taking the school ahead.

One of the senior English teachers of the school had been identified early on in the school as one who had a lot of competence in her subject but a lack of coordination and cooperation with her fellow teachers. She was convinced that what she did in the classroom and how she did it, was the best way of teaching. Besides, she continued to believe that she was doing it successfully for years and that must be the reason why it should go on, unchallenged and unexamined. Her interaction with the students was rough-edged and she remained a very traditional teacher, sitting while teaching, with a completely lackadaisical expression, threatening the students to make them fall in line and being uncooperative towards parents if they came with any grievances.

I knew we had a star performer in hand but perhaps the school had given up on her for her fixed ways of working. I started observing her classes and gave her genuine feedback, often encouraging her for what she knew but reminding her gently that she could use better instructional methods that were inclusive and empathetic. She was entrusted with some more pedagogical responsibilities which she took with scepticism initially, but being the perfectionist that she is, discharged them very well. Perhaps, for the first time in her career, she discovered her own strengths, resulting in her self-esteem rising. Last year, she received a state award from the Delhi government, which motivated her further. When she found how the entire school cheered for her and supported her for bringing her abilities in the spotlight, she started becoming one of the strong pillars of the school faculty. All these years, she was only wasted as another 'also-ran' teacher who worked as the 'way things are here', but this persistent intervention turned her into a more evolved as well as involved teacher.

One of the key features of instructional principals is that they are great teachers themselves. When teachers observe the principal teaching with excellence, they look up to the role model and are motivated to emulate what they see. Noting that the principal has a deep knowledge of the subject and keeps abreast with new developments, researching on specific topics and sharing knowledge with teachers, they observe that he/she not only supports them but also actively participates in staff development activities, such as taking part in training and workshops. Therefore, teachers feel a greater commitment to their calling.

It has often been seen in some schools that teacher training is directly outsourced and the number of hours of training become more important than the actual takeaway from such developmental activity. Teachers know they just have to sit through the programme as they would never be asked by the school leader about what they learnt and how they would bring their learning into instructional practice. On the other hand, instructional leaders develop non-threatening partnerships with teachers that are characterized by trust, openness towards the new and freedom to make mistakes, only to learn from them. Teachers also feel genuinely encouraged when a free exchange of ideas between the principal and them takes place in such programmes, contributing to meaningful interactions. That builds a culture of inquiry and change. Also, such leaders recognize time as a precious resource and instil orderliness and discipline in the school with clear timetables. As resource providers, they carefully consider all requests and act as a bridge between teachers' requirements and the management. Working with the school budget themselves, they recognize the value of the curriculum, training and school activities. It is important for instructional leaders to be able to analyse how resources can be obtained and managed.

Instructional principals' leadership is directed towards creating a commitment to purpose and they remain aware of symbolic actions to build a creative organizational climate. These leaders bring to the school a sense of drama that permits people to rise above the daily routine, to break the monotony into something more lively and vibrant. The school then starts getting its identity from such a principal. The incidence of interpersonal conflicts in such organizations becomes minimal since the principal enjoys the position of a larger-than-life persona, ensuring that teachers remain aware of it.

Instructional leaders are able to assess the strengths and weaknesses of the team members (teachers) and manage them well by integrating personal and organizational goals for them to be able to operate at a higher level. They are liberal in their appreciation of teachers, building further upon positive strokes. Acknowledging the contribution of the staff is a regular practice by such principals. Moreover, when the principal is impartial in dealing with the complaints from students and teachers, it sets a positive tone for the school. Instructional leaders 'hold up a mirror' and serve as 'another set of eyes' for teachers by engaging in thoughtful discourse. Using inquiry and offering appreciation to teachers, they are able to push the envelope to strive for excellence, enhancing the effects on teachers, emotionally, cognitively and behaviourally.

In conclusion, it can be said that instructional leadership is second only to classroom instruction among all school-related factors that contribute to what and how students learn in the school.

# 2

# The Apex of the School Pyramid

Anyone who visits a large school gets confounded by its startling complexity, often wondering how to navigate it. Large schools are so multi-tiered that the accountability, autonomy, collaboration and coordination functions get inextricably intertwined—intensively. The junior wing, the primary wing, the middle school and the senior school are just a few of the spaces to be navigated on a daily basis in such schools. Visitors often fill up forms at the front office, so that they could be directed to the right person to address their issues. Sometimes, there is chaotic centralization and at times there is unfathomable decentralization. Some educational institutions prefer to be rigidly hierarchal while others try to flatten the control and command structure. There is no single monolithic structure in schools; therefore, how the leadership flows through the maze of their labyrinth remains complex. How much of teacher agency is there in the school, what the role of the school coordinator is, and how the principal guides and directs the school stakeholders, cutting through the steps of hierarchy, are some of the questions that need to be answered.

Hierarchy is a way to structure an organization using different levels of authority within a group of individuals. The person with the most formal authority is at the top of the hierarchy. The amount of power decreases as one moves down the hierarchy. The hierarchy in a school's pyramid structure begins with the principal at the apex, followed by the vice principal or deputy head, then coordinators, in charges, class representatives, all buttressed by the supporting base of teachers (Fig. 2). This top-down model of leadership is often looked at pejoratively and is considered

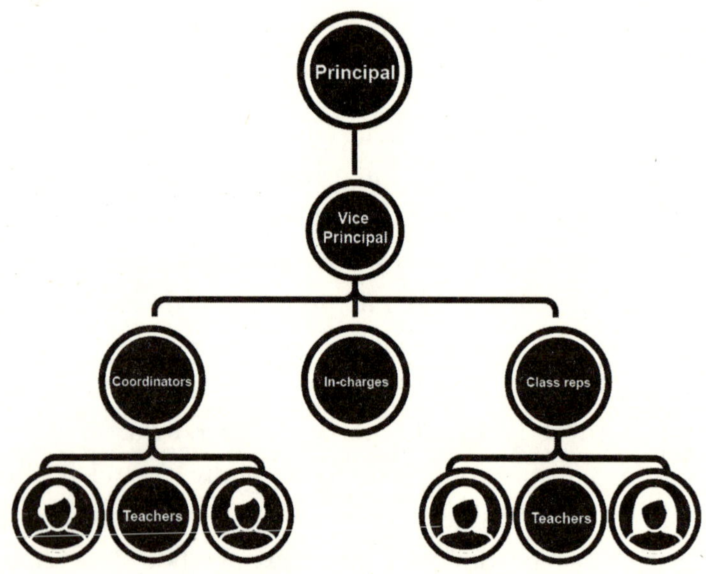


**Fig. 2: Hierarchical Leadership**

as an affront to the autonomy of educators. It is widely accepted that quality initiatives will not occur unless there is a buy-in, a willingness of those engaged in implementing them. Without this buy-in, there is a possibility of resentful compliance that dooms the initiative to inevitable failure. Principals who actually foster the creation of a learning organization are well-advised by experience and educational research to build widespread consensus, before proceeding.

Someone has to decide the 'How', 'What', 'When', 'Why' in the school and also the 'If' pertaining to the school growth and development. Clearly, a laissez-faire system will run aground without showing any sustained and substantive achievement. What then is the concept referred to as 'directed empowerment' by author Robert Waterman who was a consultant with McKinsey and Co. and is currently the director of the Waterman Group management consulting firm. He noted that strong organizational cultures yield strong companies. Organizational culture develops from shared assumptions, beliefs and values exhibited explicitly and implicitly.

With Thomas Peters, Waterman developed the McKinsey's 7S Model to link strategy and organizational effectiveness. The seven elements included Strategy, Structure, Systems, Shared Values, Skills, Style and Staff. When integrated, these elements have the power to lead organizations to success. However, for such a strong culture to emerge, there must be alignment with the organization's strategic context and the ability to adapt to environmental changes. When values are shared, they lead to improved performance of the organization.

In today's highly competitive educational climate, more dynamic than in any preceding era, the only constant is change. Schools have to continually reinvent themselves to stay ahead of competitors. There are leaders who move from strength to strength, adjusting to the changing expectations to maintain excellence through the process of renewal. These leaders make strategic decisions as informed optimists. They identify issues much before others can, believe in communication and reinforce their decisions creatively. Renewing leaders have a voracious hunger for facts and information, remaining open, curious and inquisitive, fearlessly securing teacher commitment with their creative inputs. They know how to keep things moving with their visible attention. With the positional authority they have, they continue to goad their followers to keep moving in the desired direction, their directed empowerment exponentially lending a competitive edge to their organization.

The 'Culture of Discipline', a concept developed by Jim Collins, author and business expert, is another cornerstone that creates exceptional organizations within the hierarchal framework. In schools led by leaders who take disciplined action within the framework of accountability, teachers do not have jobs—instead, they have responsibilities. Such leaders create order out of chaos by promoting awareness of emerging trends and potential problems. They lead with questions, not by giving answers. Their belief in dialogue and debate overrides the conviction of others that coercion delivers results. With their positional authority, they get the right people to work, and with their fierce resolve to do whatever it takes, they get the entire organization moving towards excellence. They never fail to give due credit to those who work diligently to achieve the desired results. When you have disciplined people, you don't need hierarchy and when you have disciplined thought, you don't need bureaucracy. When you have disciplined action, you don't need excessive controls. Leaders who blend a culture of discipline with an ethic of entrepreneurship create a magical alchemy, resulting in superior performance.

It could thus be said that hierarchical leadership is not a negative connotation of leadership. Effective leaders also recognize that the improvement of school management cannot wait for everyone in the organization to have a favourable attitude towards the proposed change. There is abundant evidence in the field of psychology, organizational behaviour and education, that changes in attitudes follow rather than precede the changes in behaviour. One of the most essential prerequisites of leadership is clarity—when the school stakeholders see that clarity every day in their routine, there is no scope left for ambiguity. When leaders call upon teachers to accomplish what they have been asked to achieve, then they create structures for making it possible. There are leaders who work as servant leaders, asking themselves what they can give to the organization in the form of tools and skills to ensure that desired success. They are emphatically assertive when required and use the power of their position to get people to act in ways that are aligned with the mission of higher levels of learning for all.

But just as everything has two sides, it must also be remembered that a positional authority vested in a controlling person could lead to a lot of disruption in the organization. There are many examples of schools with a hierarchical leadership that have led to power struggles in the system. They do not take kindly to even legitimate objections and crush all dialogue, failing to address the concerns raised by teachers or students. One of the schools, where I began working soon after completing my BEd, had such a leader at the helm who enjoyed an unchallenged position in the organization. The positional authority that he had attained was getting misused for meeting his personal agenda rather than organizational growth. Most teachers could never gain access to the principal's office since there were clear-cut tiers of structures. Problems were allowed to fester for long since one had to go through various channels of authority, each one looking at the issues at their own time and according to their whims. Having no direct contact with the principal meant that neither did reports on the good work of the teachers reach the principal nor on any functional lapse. The departmental heads met with the principal to apprise him of the daily goings-on. That often led to filtering of information as it suited the person concerned. Parents also couldn't meet with the principal even in the direst of situations since they were directed to the coordinators first. Clearly, the numerous steps of hierarchy in the school kept the principal out of the loop of everyday situations.

The case of the Singapore education system can be brought in here. In the country, education is seen as crucial to building national identity and developing national citizenry with the social and economic development that has taken Singapore from a Third World country to a First World state in less than 40 years. Singapore is renowned for its students' outstanding performances in international tests such as the Trends in International Mathematics and Science Study (TIMMS) and the Programme for International

Student Assessment (PISA). However, the preoccupation with students doing well in exams is no longer thought relevant to meet the demands of Singapore's 21st century knowledge-based economy. As a next step, the government has taken many measures to develop professional learning communities (PLCs) in Singapore schools to build capacity for school leaders and teachers to initiate broad-based curricular changes for the holistic development of students. The measures included continuous professional development, community learning, job-embedded learning with reflective, evidence-informed and inquiry-based practice. With regard to school autonomy, emphasis was placed on the self-evaluation of teachers and leaders. In 2005, the Ministry of Education mandated one hour per week of curricular time for teachers and leaders to engage in professional dialogues on school-based innovations. Engagement in rigorous reflection, use of research and wisdom, collaborative experiments with new teaching and assessment practices were encouraged, in a hitherto centralized top-down system.

The hierarchical top-down structure of Singapore schools, with the principal at the helm, traditionally ensures strong and direct alignment between the stages of policy conception to implementation. This requires a shift in the pattern of power and influence both within and among schools in relation to the centre. A research study was conducted in 2012 to understand how PLCs, mainly a Western concept in the structure and set of practices, evolved to match with the hierarchical context of Singapore schools that had centralized 'command and control' systems. It was found that PLCs remained confined to pedagogical practices, subject expertise and student learning. Teacher agency, principal empowerment and autonomy remained restricted. Most important decisions were still taken by the government and no flexibility came to the school structures. Another major study conducted earlier in 2009 found that Singapore schools still remained highly reliant on formal didactic teaching, rote learning and summative testing. It could be said in conclusion that in schools characterized by greater devolution of authority, PLCs develop effectively for the whole school improvement. In hierarchical structures, instead of becoming transformational, PLCs remain confined to classroom teaching and subject expertise.

Whether it is about leadership of a school or a country, it is possible to find relevant nuggets from different experiences. Here is a real example as narrated by a teacher of a school. One Saturday afternoon, word came from the principal's office that a report was 'urgently required' by Monday morning. That set the entire staff working overtime, since there was a culture of delivering on the deadline. Relevant data was quickly assembled and reviewed, rechecking of numbers done and organizing of the data into graphs was finally achieved. In the process, the school remained open on Sunday for many teachers and departmental heads to come and work on the report. Finally, a perfectly bound excellent report was produced by Monday morning for the principal's perusal. Days passed, but the report remained lying on the side table in the principal's office till the vice principal reminded her that the staff was anxiously waiting for her comments/remarks on the project done. By then, however, the teachers' mood had already shifted from excitement and commitment to frustration and cynicism. Actually, all that the principal wanted to know was how far the progress of the project that was underway had advanced. However, that offhand remark had percolated down the chain of command, which during its transmission had metamorphosed into an 'order' from the initial 'suggestion'! This instance shows how everything can change so dramatically in a control and command hierarchical structure. 'Subordinates' in such cultures continue to report to the 'Superiors', instead of stakeholders working in perfect coordination.

A highly pyramidical hierarchical system, therefore, despite its potential to cultivate the culture of discipline and accountability, can adversely affect the organizational members' morale and motivation, which are the key ingredients for efficient performance.

# 3

# Control Button in the Hands of the Principal

The concept of autocratic leadership stems from early experimental studies by the American social psychologists K. Lewin, R. Lippitt and R.K. White in 1939. Fairly specific hypotheses and theories concerning interpersonal influence and leadership began to be systematically investigated by them. The modern operationalization of autocratic leadership later by social scientists Rob Foels and Arthur G. Jago characterized autocratic behaviour as centralized decision-making and heavy concentration of power, through which the leader controls every aspect of the subordinate's activity without any consideration. All decision-making and policy implementation are unilateral and hierarchical. Power sharing is anathema to such leaders, fostering discontent and hostility. Such an organizational climate may encourage members to only promote themselves and work on impression management strategies. Consequently, power struggles do not accept the hierarchy with arbitrary expectations about rank-appropriate roles. There are a large number of schools where autocratic leadership is a way of life. The school processes and systems revolve only around the leader's position and disposition. Intrinsic motivation is absent from such schools and all that gets done every day is the routine task.

An organization's functioning depends to a large extent on how happy and motivated its members feel to pursue the collective welfare. Leadership literature generally identifies autocratic leadership as one entity, not taking care of the socio-emotional dimensions of the group cohesion. They are particularly low on the factor of consideration, which is strongly related to job satisfaction, motivation and effectiveness. That can negatively influence group stability and effectiveness. Being control freaks, they are wary of discussions while taking decisions in the group. Such leaders, then, naturally discourage their followers' loyalty and dedication towards the organization. This situation is experienced more in private sectors but may also reflect in government schools. Autocratic leaders consciously or unconsciously, overtly or covertly try to attain their organizational goals at any cost. In the school field, such research wasn't conducted till the last decade or so. There are a plethora of anecdotal cases where teachers have suffered harassment, intimidation, pressure, force and psychological violence. In 2014, I established a school at Hisar for which everything was raised from scratch. The building was still under construction when I joined, the admission process had to begin and teachers recruited, trained and inducted into the system. The school chairman, an erstwhile electrical shop owner who used his money to build the school, had absolutely no clue about education. After the school successfully started functioning in a few months, I was called for an emergency meeting with some teachers, late in the evening. We all reached his office where he gave everyone a dressing down and flailed a notebook before my eyes, then asked me if this was the school I was leading. A teacher had incorrectly marked an answer for Grade 4. I felt embarrassed since I was sitting with the same teachers I had been training for months. I tried reasoning with him that this was just a human error and we could speak with the parent. However, he wouldn't have any of it and asked us if we really deserved the salary he was giving. That was the evening when I resigned from the post and left the city within a few days. I realized that it would be difficult to give leadership lessons to a person who indulges in aggressive, humiliating and unethical behaviour. Not only did the entire organization get demoralized, besides the teacher who had wrongly marked an incorrect answer, but it also showed future forebodings for the school. Such a leadership style destroys the self-esteem and confidence of teachers.

Such a leader demands unconditional servitude without engaging in any debate or reasoning. The same chairman asked me to make the school timetable in such a way that each student would learn at least three foreign languages. I was utterly shocked and tried explaining to him that in this city, even English was no less than a foreign language, so how would we ever teach three more foreign languages? However, he wouldn't hear of it and teachers for French, German and Spanish were appointed, much against my wish. The students, many of whom were coming from rural areas, were struggling already with English and now they had to learn languages that were alien to them. Teachers were also appointed, since monetary resources were never a constraint. What was truly in short supply was the vision and purpose of education in this case. The students for whom the school was established, continued to study with great strain and teachers weren't able to produce the results that were expected of them. The entire school had become a place of low morale and motivation since each teacher was struggling with various languages. It was a foregone conclusion that if the school chairman has some dated and fixated ideas about education—or rather, lack of ideas—it was futile to make any progress. It is obvious that such a climate in a school may not lead to any team work or academic achievement. It was also clear in the case of this school that we were dealing with a self-proclaimed educationist whose own ego was far too big to be able to see anything beyond his nose. Now, each one of the teachers appointed at the time the school was established has left and the attrition continues to be high.

One-way organizational communication destroys teachers' perspective and ideas, leading to a greater incidence of organizational conflicts. The negative influence of such leaders is all too pervasive and visible. The stress levels of teachers remain high at such a workplace and they prefer to toe the line instead of challenging the old traditional systems and methods to bring in innovations. It is not surprising then that many experienced and competent teachers leave such an organization since their work is never appreciated or acknowledged. Not only are the attrition rates too high but teachers' efficiency and commitment are too low. Such a controlling style of leading the school leads to a highly structured environment for teaching and learning where neither students nor teachers have self-directed and self-regulated attitudes towards teaching and learning. They have no role in decision-making and are only seen as cogs of the machinery which has to constantly move. Lack of connectedness breeds complete isolation and loneliness among teachers and the community fabric gets torn. Clearly, such organizations are lowest in encouraging trust (Fig. 3).

Here, I would like to recall an incident. As the head of the department of geography in a school, I met with the principal, seeking permission to take the students of various

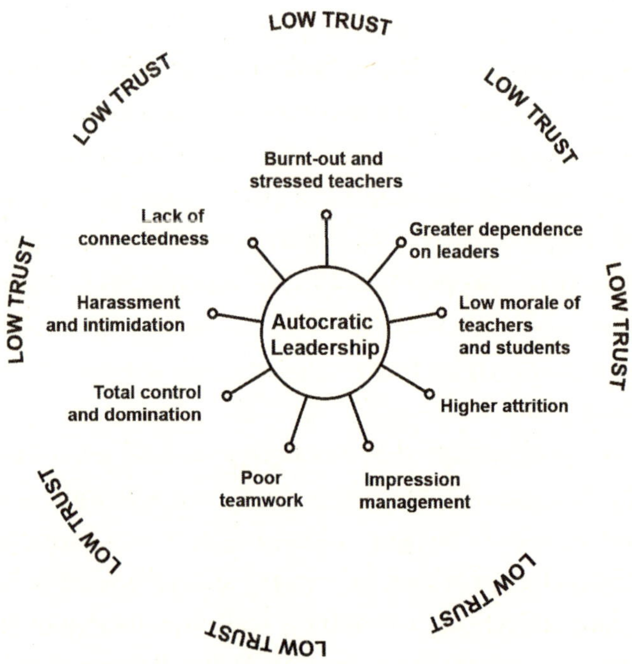


**Fig. 3: Autocratic Leadership**

classes just across the school to show them how harvesting takes place and what kind of machines are used for the task. It was the end of the Rabi season and the students were studying topics pertaining to agriculture, ranging from sowing seasons, field practices, mechanized farming and so on. What could have been a better opportunity for the students to see these activities directly? However, the school calendar did not list the said activity for the day. Mine was only an impromptu decision but wonderfully spontaneous—teachers are always on the lookout for such learning opportunities. The principal refused since the school policy had no leeway even for the slightest of deviation from the fixed annual calendar. It not only disappointed the teacher but also the students who could have seen for themselves how the practices of harvesting and threshing take place. It was futile to argue with the principal that the harvesting season comes only at a certain time of the year and it wouldn't harm any schedule if some practical and experiential learning took place. Clearly, there was a gap between what was said in the principal's speeches and what actually was permitted in the school. Such autocratic leadership kills all excitement and enthusiasm in schools and their teachers refrain from venturing into spontaneity in the teaching process.

The above-mentioned example could be corroborated by the findings of a descriptive study that was conducted in Turkey in which the population of the study consisted of 6,125 teachers working in primary and secondary schools. For data collection, a mobbing scale was used which was developed by researchers Antonio Aiello, Patrizia Deitinger, Christian Nardella and Michela Bonafede in 2008, later adapted into Turkish by A.Laleoglu and E. Ozmete in 2013. Teachers were assessed at four dimensions—relations, threat, barriers in work and commitment. Factor analysis along with statistical tools such as the t-test and analysis of variance (ANOVA) were used to analyse the data collected. The findings revealed that there was a significant relationship between autocratic leadership and teachers' feeling of being under threat and experiencing harassment. It was also seen to have the highest predictive power on barriers pertaining to work. The relations with colleagues were also negatively affected by the autocratic leadership. Besides, there was an increasing feeling of burnout among teachers since the levels of motivation remained low. Poor job satisfaction, absence of organizational citizenship and reluctance to work were other outcomes found in the schools with autocratic leadership.

Clearly, teachers' morale in such schools gets eroded and chipped away. If they are constantly told that they are failing, they start believing that they are failing indeed! It is next to impossible to develop professional learning communities in such schools, owing to the absence of meaningful dialogue and multipronged interactions. Unpredictability, conflict and dissent happen on a daily basis in such schools, reducing the time for school improvement. It is rare to find new leaders emerging from such organizations since there is no culture of empowerment. Autocratic leader believe that teachers are weak, unwilling to work, incapable of self-determination with limited reasoning ability. They never involve teachers in group participation and collective decisions. Tasks are assigned without consultation and the leader expects acceptance without questioning.

The fact that leadership is a group process and followers play a key role in leadership is ignored by autocratic leaders. Feelings of uncertainty remain too high in such schools. Since organizational functioning depends to a large extent on how motivated its members feel to pursue the collective welfare, the feeling of entitativity remains low under autocratic leadership. Teachers do not identify with the collective goals and vision and remain unwilling to self-sacrifice for the larger good of the school. Loyalty and dedication remain missing, and connectedness totally absent.

The demoralizing impact could be far and wide, and all-pervading in the school. Owing to the absence of psychological safety among teachers, the team performance remains subpar. Teachers do not feel that situations are secure, predictable and clear. There is a large body of research to prove that a team's perceived sense of security has a profound impact on its performance. Power struggles continue to dominate the organization, curtailing any innovation and team spirit. One of the schools where I was guiding the teachers' professional development had two campuses, geographically separate but within the same city. The junior wing was led by the headmistress who had been associated with the school from its inception. The senior wing of the school had a principal who rose to the position after being a vice principal for many years in the same school. The two heads of the school remained mired in power struggles to such an extent that the different parts of the school did not look or work like the same school with a common vision and mission. Both the leaders wanted to establish their supremacy, forgetting the fact that they were expected to lead the school with commitment and devotion.

They neither cooperated with each other nor saw eye to eye. Over a period of time, teachers started getting divided into well-established camps where hostility towards the other side became so profound that it started reflecting on the working of the school. Since I was dealing with both the branches to guide teachers on their professional development, I often found myself embroiled in utterly wasteful discussions, which instead of focusing on teachers' growth, remained confined to power struggles. The school chairman had to intervene to restore some semblance of normalcy. However, both the leaders refused to relent until finally one had to be asked to leave. This is how a brilliant opportunity to lead a school was lost, owing to such unnecessary skirmishes.

Teachers' feeling of job satisfaction is also directly related to the leadership style in a school, as a study conducted in Nigerian Secondary Schools in 2012 reveals. In this descriptive study, 28 public secondary schools participated, from which a sample of 280 teachers responded to a survey. The purpose of this study was to investigate the influence of the principal's leadership style on teachers' job satisfaction. Data collected were analysed using mean and standard deviation values. The findings clearly revealed that the principal's attitude of not considering teachers' suggestions and ideas in decision-making makes teachers lose interest in their job. Their contribution towards administration becomes minimal and all that they do is routine teaching in the classroom. The leader's strict insistence on teachers' absolute obedience and compliance can even lead to teacher insubordination. Academic productivity remains low and a supervisory system in the school causes undesirable behaviour on the part of teachers. Cordial socialization and communication, which are essential for effective organizational performance, get restricted under such leaders. The study further reveals that democratic leadership enhances job satisfaction since it makes place for teachers' opinions, comments and suggestions. The study recommended that principals should undergo in-service and refresher courses on the modern rudiments of leadership style.

Clearly, considerate behaviour of leaders, oriented towards maintaining good interpersonal relations and a supportive work culture, achieves better results than authoritarian leadership.

# 4

# Using Social Exchange to Achieve Short-term Results

Theories of leadership have been in a state of ferment for decades. Proposed theories have been based upon the structure of the organization, needs of the people who work in it, the environment in which the organization operates and the particular situations faced by its leaders. Most of the leadership theories have judged the worth of a leader based upon his/her ability to take the organization from point A to point B. In 1985, Bernard M. Bass, the renowned American scholar credited with laying the foundations of organizational psychology, proposed a new model of leadership, based on the work of leadership expert James MacGregor Burns, in which he described leaders as transformational or transactional. Burns first introduced the concept of transforming leadership in his descriptive research on political leaders. According to Burns, leaders and followers help each other to advance to a higher level of morale and motivation. He established the concepts of 'transforming' and 'transactional' leadership. While transforming leadership creates significant change in the life of people and organizations, transactional leadership is a 'give and take' relationship between leaders and followers. Transactional leaders do not strive for cultural change in the organization but work in the existing culture. Bass extended the work of Burns by explaining the psychological mechanisms that underlie transforming and transactional leadership. In contrast to Burns, Bass suggested that leadership can simultaneously display both transformational and transactional leadership.

Bass theorized that there is a certain kind of leader who is capable of inspiring subordinates to heights they have never dreamed of. He referred to this leader as transformational. The transactional leader, on the other hand, according to Bass, is rooted in a two-way influence—a social exchange in which the leader gives something and gets something in return. The two factors identified for transactional relationship were contingent reward and management by exception (Fig. 4). In transactional leadership, there is a social exchange in which both the leader and the follower give something and get something in return. This is based on the reinforcement theory of motivation proposed by psychologist B.F. Skinner. It states that the individual's behaviour is a function of its consequences. It is based on the 'law of effect' which suggests that a person's behaviour with positive consequences tends to be repeated while that with negative consequences does not. Thus, in a transactional relationship, both parties agree to what is to be done in order to receive a reward or to avoid punishment. Positive

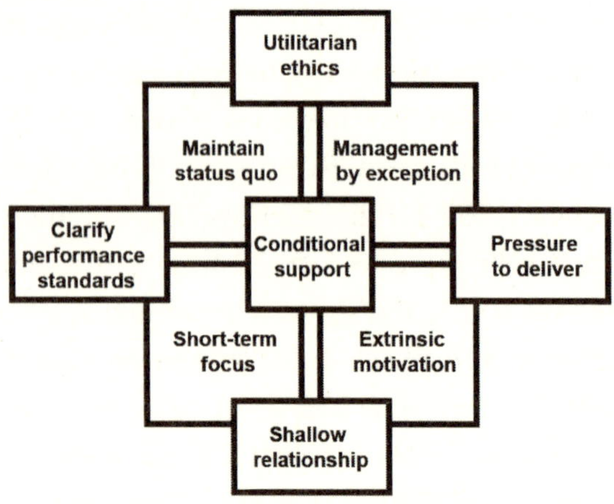


**Fig. 4: Transactional Leadership**

reinforcement stimulates occurrence of a behaviour. The more spontaneous the giving of a reward is, the greater reinforcement value it has. When undesirable consequences are applied for showing disapproval of a certain behaviour, it acts as a deterrent for future occurrence of the negative behaviour.

Transactional leaders set goals, clarify performance standards, tell people what to do and how to do it, reward good workers and reprimand the poor ones. As long as the performance standards are met with, the transactional leader remains uninvolved. It is only when the performance falls below expected standards that the leader intervenes. This intervention is often negative. Transactional leaders have task-oriented goals for which they tend to focus on task completion and employee compliance. They rely heavily on organizational rewards and punishments to influence employee performance. Similar to this tenet, management by exception was defined by Lester R. Bittel, the globally renowned authority on management and supervision, as a system of identification and communication that signals to the manager when his attention is required. When no attention is needed, he remains silent. This approach to leadership was based on the scientific management theory of Fredrick Taylor, a pioneer in scientific management that emphasized the role and responsibility of managers to guide workers in how to do their work and to provide the tools and training for this, and was primarily designed to save executives' time to focus on high-value work. Transactional leaders focus on the basic needs of their staff, not on building high motivation levels or achieving job satisfaction for employees. It is commonplace to find such a model of leadership in schools where pressures to deliver on the management-set goals are prominent and non-negotiable.

Here, I would like to mention the tremendous stress under which the principal and the teachers of a school work—stress being a dominant factor in many schools which are wanting in ethics. The principal's remuneration is based on the number of admissions that take place every year, a preset target. Irrespective of how admissions happen in the school, the principal is obliged to bring in profits to the school coffers as a part of his/her duty. Not surprising then, that the proverbial Damocles' sword continues to dangle over the school principal, with all his/her time and efforts spent on this single most important target. This takes away the time which could be spent on instructional and pedagogical leadership, the job satisfaction of teachers as well as their commitment and motivation. In such schools, academic pursuits and the overall development of students which should be the core of a school system, take a back seat. Also, there are many schools where the results delivered by the outgoing board classes are considered the sole purpose of the school leader's work. When only the school ranking, league tables, comparative results analysis with other schools in the city and the country become the criteria for school success, then, clearly, it is a transactional association between the management and the leadership of the school. It is not surprising, therefore, that such leaders complete required tasks, maintain the status quo in the organization, direct teachers to achieve established goals and avoid any unnecessary risk.

The growing expectations of the management with a lopsided view of the purpose of education affects the thoughts, strategies, beliefs and philosophy of the school leadership in the current competitive climate of schools. Rapid developments experienced in the internal and external environments where the schools operate have a deep influence on all the role expectations of the school leader. It is imperative that the adaptation of school principals to the changing management and social structure is treated as a crucial necessity. However, the trade-off between expectations and moral responsibility of an educational institution has to be kept in mind. It looks like a tall order for the principals to be charismatic, well-informed, virtuous and visionary, but are these qualities not the imperative features of school leadership in the natural course? If the hurdles in successful and innovative school administration hamper the very necessity of raising the overall standards of the school, then it could be a matter of worry.

Transactional expectations impede the transformational work of school principals. A healthy and intellectually stimulating environment in the school can only be created when motivation runs high across the school stakeholders. To convey and work for the philosophy, mission and objectives of the school, the principal needs to be freed to competently steer the ship by being at the helm. To inculcate a deep team spirit, build innovative culture and empower school teachers, leaders need to be trusted themselves. Inspirational motivation comes from inspired and enthused leaders. They need to identify possibilities and capabilities of each teacher to set objectives for themselves. Conditional support and awards do not go a long way in building an enabling culture. Innovations, entrepreneurship, reforms and continuous development are the obligations in today's competitive world but to achieve this, principals have to establish a relational trust with all the teachers.

Recognizing everyone's contribution and appreciating their performance will have a lasting impact on the school rather than a culture of rigid expectations without an iota of empathy for the team. Transactional leaders look at the members only as a tool to achieve the set goals in today's dizzyingly fast-changing educational environment. The critical task of training and development of teachers to make them self-aware and strong pedagogues is unconditionally a principal's task. A leadership style which focuses on the few who deliver on the set goals while ignoring or reprimanding the others who do not, builds a divided organization. The latter group of teachers do not find any reason to be innovative when they notice the absence of encouragement for the same. When deficiencies are highlighted and achievements are ignored, it creates a culture of apathy and shallow relationships in the organization.

In one of the schools where I was leading the teacher professional development programme, I used to discuss the training needs of teachers with the coordinator for hours. During these discussions, I was told that teachers are mortally afraid of being called out if they make any lapses. Whatever good work they do is conveniently ignored by the principal while mistakes are highlighted. Since the discussions also took place with the principal, I often asked him why teachers never get appreciated, to which he replied that good work is its own reward. Teachers are responsible adults and they could not be treated like students. However, if he wouldn't point out the mistakes, would they not be repeated by others? When I asked the principal if he appreciates and incentivizes the achievements of teachers, would they also not be repeated by the others? A public recognition, a word of appreciation, some reward—they all have the wherewithal to get the similar actions replicated. However, when policing the school is the culture prevalent, how do long-term changes occur in the school? Teachers are even afraid of smiling at each other in the school, fearing that it might get misconstrued as a lackadaisical attitude towards work. No wonder then, the school in question, continues to work with the policy of strict supervision, achieving everyday goals—but it is a matter of debate whether it will have any far-sighted vision for the school development.

While taking over the leadership of the last school I worked in, I was pleasantly surprised at how teachers reacted to the appreciation they received on successfully accomplishing and completing a task given to them. I had initiated it as a regular exercise in the school to publicly acknowledge—through the written word—the efforts made by various individuals. I hoped it would give the recipients a boost in their morale and strength to their endeavour. Gradually, I came to know that teachers eagerly waited to get this public recognition, which meant that the appreciation communique sent to the staff would become a talking point for many days after it was sent. On inquiring about this, I was told by the vice principal and many others that they had never before got this recognition in spite of working hard to achieve goals. The principal would only convey her displeasure over lapses but refrained from appreciation for any achievement, however important it was. Teachers were content with their lot then, since they had never known any other way, accepting the culture of highlighting shortcomings but never praising teachers for the incredible feats they achieved. Clearly, that was a typical case of transactional leadership.

A research study was conducted in 2001 for 45 private secondary schools in the USA to determine the headmasters' leadership qualities. A multifactor leadership questionnaire was administered to find out if the same transformational and transactional factors found among military and business leaders appear among secondary school headmasters. The factors taken into consideration for the questionnaire were charisma, individualized consideration, intellectual stimulation, contingent reward and management by exception. In the survey findings, transactional factors correlated far less strongly with teacher satisfaction and effectiveness. A culture of contingent reward and management by exception wherein good leaders were acknowledged while the ineffective leaders were reprimanded, did not have any impact on job satisfaction in schools. Clearly, job satisfaction and leaders' effectiveness have a much higher correlation with the traits of transformational leadership. Transactional leaders stay at the lower levels of Maslow's Needs Hierarchy as compared to transformational leaders who reach the levels of self-actualization and carry the rest of the team ahead. Maslow's hierarchy of needs states that physiological safety, love and belonging, esteem and self-actualization needs dictate individuals' behaviour and motivate them if met. Transactional leaders neither relate empathetically nor intuitively with their followers. The 'carrot and stick' method of leading does not transcend team members' self-interest for the sake of the entire group.

There is an ethical dimension to leadership which is linked with the question of whether what is being done as well as the means employed to do it are morally legitimate. Educational management scholars consider ethics and morals as a fundamental part of the essence of being an educational leader. When school leaders explore a given ethical dilemma using several ethical perspectives, the best solution is reached. However, transactional leaders often fall short of the ethics of care, profession, fairness and critique. An example here would illustrate how teachers' ethics can dictate the procedures in the school. As the head of department of geography, I also worked closely with the head of department of history. She was one of the pioneering teachers of the school and her children also studied in the same school, just as mine did. As I used to teach her daughter too, I was cautioned by my fellow teachers to ensure that no harsh word was ever spoken to her daughter, even in the gravest of infringements. It was clear that special treatment was meted out to her by all the teachers. The student in question also knew that and enjoyed the special privileges given to her. Thankfully, I never had to deal with her for any disciplinary matter since where I stood about the standards of integrity would be clear. But very soon, I came face to face with a disturbing incident in the school. As the middle school coordinator, I was responsible to ensure that the timetable functioned smoothly, exams took place under proper supervision and invigilation, and the students attended the classes regularly. However, while I was taking some routine rounds of the building, the timetable in charge told me that some Grade 10 students had been found near the canteen, skipping classes and chatting in the courtyard. When I went there, I was shocked to see my daughter among the students. When she saw me approaching, she hung her head in shame. I felt tearful since this was the last thing I ever expected in the school. My daughter was a sincere and conscientious student, doing very well in academics. But adolescents do have their own whims and fancies and schools have to deal with them responsibly. The procedural method in such cases was that the parents were called for counselling with the principal and they had to be given a letter of warning. Not even for a moment, did I face any dilemma, social or emotional. The letters were made for all the students and sent to their parents through them. They had to meet with the principal the next day.

One could imagine my plight when I received the letter by my daughter in the evening. She wanted to take a day off to avoid more embarrassment. However, she was told to attend the school and face the consequences. After the principal had met with all the parents, separately, in my presence, I continued to sit before the principal and told him that this girl was my child, fighting back my tears. Needless to say, it was a distressing moment for me, having worked in the school for long with the highest standards of professionalism and dignity. The principal seemed too shocked for words and he said that it was alright and these things happen. The news spread like wildfire that the coordinator's daughter was one among the students who bunked the classes.

Teachers came to meet me to inquire about the incident—some to extend sympathy while some clearly enjoyed my discomfort. However, it was clear to everyone that there are no discriminatory policies for anyone so far as I was concerned. The stark contrast in ethics between the heads of the geography and history departments stood in all its clarity. However, I felt stronger and found myself getting more respect from the colleagues and the school authorities. Clearly, ethics do not change with the kinship or choices.

The single-minded focus on the objectives given to teachers leads transactional leaders to emphasize only the procedural treatment of organizational functions. Their decision-making is not comprehensive since multiple inputs with various options are not considered. As the moral obligation to help others without any expected personal benefit is missing, the sense of social responsibility remains low. This can be seen in many schools today, particularly since the students from economically weaker sections study with the students from privileged backgrounds. Teachers could often be judgemental on the students of the economically weaker sections (EWS), quick to reprimand them for even the slightest of infraction and jumping to unfair conclusions when there is a scuffle or an argument between the privileged students and their EWS counterparts.

It is truly tragic to meet parents who request that their child should not be sitting alongside the EWS child. I have often spent hours discussing with them the implications of their thought process on their child's psyche. Once such attitudes are formed, they may last for a lifetime. Many schools admit these EWS students only as their perfunctory responsibility, never really understanding their world and attitudes.

Professional judgement based on deep knowledge and expertise is not generally found in transactional leaders, as utilitarian ethics take precedence in each of their actions. Since transactional leaders rely on rules and regulations, with the emphasis on procedural fairness, they do not consider multiple options to reach the school goals. Focused more on structures and processes, they often ignore the human element and moral reasoning. Standard setting and monitoring of performance are very prominent in their scheme of things. However, that can be a strength in case of schools where a laissez-faire leadership system has been the norm for long, throwing things into disarray. Their pragmatic approach towards every task can move people to believe in the leadership in such schools.

An example of the centralized state education system in Israel can be very illustrative here. The system is built on the tight hold on fiscal, administrative, organizational, pedagogical and structural features of public schooling. However, with time, the public education system changed with the introduction of market and privatization policies promoting autonomous schools, parental choice and national standardizing testing.

A research study covering several academic institutions, with a sample of 248 participants enrolled in the Master's degree programme was conducted in Israel. Graduate programmes in educational administration in Israel serve mostly aspiring principals who are acting school leaders, with 75 per cent of these participants holding mid-level management positions. A multifactor leadership questionnaire (MLQ) was administered with factors of transformational and transactional leadership traits. Bivariate correlational analysis revealed that transformational leaders significantly used ethical activism (i.e., critique, care and profession) while transactional leaders significantly used ethical conformism (i.e., fairness, utilitarianism and community). Thus, this work provides support for the moral view of transactional school leaders committed to ethical conformism through a pragmatic utilitarian approach that considers the welfare and interests of all individuals affected by their decisions.

Clearly, transactional leadership minimizes workplace anxiety and concentrates on clear organizational objectives. It eliminates confusion within the chain of command, since there is a clear-cut organizational chart. Members grow in confidence as there is no ambiguity and goals are fixed.

However, creative and innovative teachers in the field of education may feel stifled by a rigid structure of transactional leadership. It eliminates individuality from the organization, impeding the free spirit of creative mindsets. The originality of teachers cannot fall within the purview of a fixed structure. It is not surprising, therefore, that such organizations are low in empathy, since teachers do not feel intrinsically motivated to achieve much higher and superior goals. Efficiency gets greater weightage than efficacy. More followers than future leaders get created under transactional leadership in such a scenario. Unless a balance is maintained, transactional leaders may just stymie the growth and thwart change for the larger good of the organization. Consistency and predictability come at the cost of innovation and dynamism, which is not what schools must strive for. At the end of the day, each school must be motivation-driven with a relentless focus on a continuous learning process.

# 5

# In Pursuit of a Higher Purpose

Leadership is an influential process between leaders and subordinates. An effective leadership is core to continuously improving the school, the principal's leadership being paramount in developing effective schools and improving student achievement. Transformational leadership is an effort to satisfy followers' needs and to move them to a higher level of work performance. The entire organization gets involved when the principal displays respect and encourages participation of all teachers. The visionary aspect of transformational leadership keeps teachers engaged with organizational goals. Such leadership increases levels of trust and satisfaction in the organization and these leaders are able to generate higher levels of effort and commitment (Fig. 5). The willingness of teachers to extend themselves to working increases their own job satisfaction. There is enough research to show that teachers feel happier with such leaders. High-functioning schools often have transformational leaders at

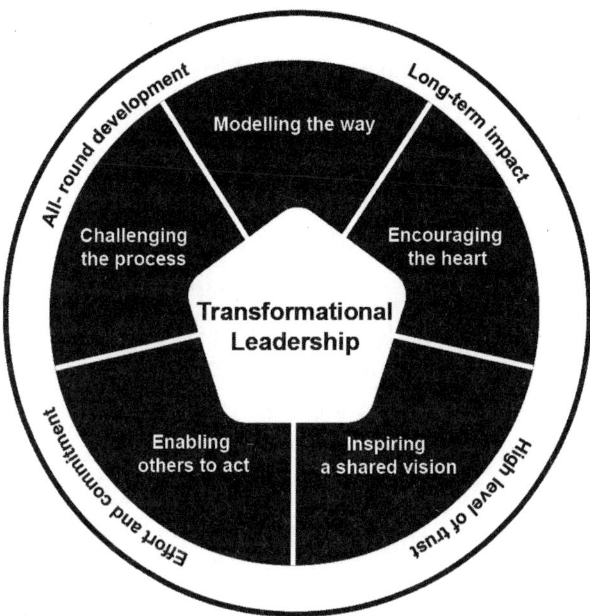


**Fig. 5: Transformational Leadership**

the helm, where the collegial environment fosters teacher empowerment. It is a powerful stimulant to all-round improvement. They build the vision in such a way that teachers willingly commit to realizing it by increasing their efficacy. Teachers are nurtured and supported by such leaders since they see role models who live the ideals propounded by them.

Various researchers have studied the influence of the principal–teacher–student achievement relationship to identify potential moderating and mediating factors. These researches have identified how leaders influence teachers and through them, the student outcomes. Over the past three decades, research in the Western world has consistently shown that school leaders, by exercising transformational leadership practices, have a positive influence on the school and student outcomes.

A large-scale study comprising many schools was undertaken by Kenneth Leithwood and Doris Jantzi to know how schools initiated reforms of their own choice as well as by the district- and state-level initiatives in Canada. Data about leadership, school and classroom conditions, student engagement and family educational culture were collected from 2465 teachers and 44,920 students from 123 elementary and junior high schools. The data was factor analysed and the main finding was that transformational leadership has strong and significant direct effects on organizational conditions. The series of three studies validates the nature of effective transformational leadership practices, teachers' decision-making, opportunities for professional development, classroom conditions and the student achievement outcomes. The results suggest that transformational school leaders are in continuous pursuit of three fundamental goals: helping staff members develop and maintain a collaborative culture, fostering teacher development and helping them solve problems together more effectively.

Innovations are easy to implement when teachers perceive their principal's transformational leadership attributes. Besides, such practices directly affect teachers' sense of well-being and quality instruction in the classroom. Transformational leaders were found communicating the school's cultural norms, values and beliefs in their day-to-day interactions with teachers, promoting continuous professional growth for everyone.

Three years back, I joined a school as principal which had the same principal since its inception 25 years ago. I noticed a few things which were not up to the standard of a good private school. It was common for students to reach late, teachers had scant respect for school bell timings, and Hindi was mostly spoken in an otherwise English medium school. These were just a few of the issues which I needed to deal with. To my utter surprise, at any hour of the school time, parents and sundry visitors could be seen walking in and out of the corridors and even classrooms, since they had never been stopped before.

In the beginning, I almost caved in under the pressure of so many loose ends that needed to be tightened up and streamlined. So I started standing at the school reception, close to the entry gates of the school, from where everyone could see me. I only nodded and smiled at all the students passing by, many looking sheepish, others embarrassed for reaching late, not to forget the parents dropping their children looking both amused and surprised. Even though the number of students arriving late was counted every day at the gate, as had been the practice for years, I thought it was a futile exercise—the sanctity of this perfunctory function was violated since late coming was the practice for more than two decades. My purpose was not to embarrass anyone but to set up a system that would be worthy of this illustrious school.

Over the next few months, it was a gargantuan task to get all teachers and students to respect school timings, without causing any damage to their self-esteem. There were protests by parents, and teachers' visible discomfort built a general climate of dissatisfaction for the next few ensuing months.

However, gradually, from more than 200 late arriving students in the beginning, the numbers started dwindling to a handful—which was an achievement by any yardstick.

Every morning, a special assembly was conducted for the students arriving late, where they were asked to sit in yoga postures and reflect on what made them arrive late to school. Some meditation exercises were done and in the end, I used to tell them motivational stories of people who achieved success against all odds by the sheer power of discipline. Clearly, I had to set the standards myself and drive home the point repeatedly that it was a non-negotiable issue when it came to building a disciplined school.

However, this measure was fraught with many problems since established cultures and ways of working take long to change. Every morning, an hour was spent only on dealing with latecomers, sometimes accompanied by their parents with all kinds of requests and reasons for their late arrival. I tried explaining to them that if the school continues to take more than 200 late arriving students every morning because each one of them had a valid reason, so to speak, classes would never start in time. The measure led to a lot of furore amongst the parent community since it had shaken everyone from their comfort zones.

To begin the process of dialogue with the parent community, I started organizing a coffee meeting with parents every week, where informal discussions took place, their issues listened to and my suggestions on discipline proffered. It took months for students and their parents to come around. However, some unpleasant incidents also happened along the way. Police officials visited us to say that the school cannot stop students from coming late if they have a valid reason. I was subjected to all kinds of pressure tactics, but I refused to relent for the larger good of the school. The school almanac was shown to the police officials where clear rules were mentioned about the school timings. They asked me how these students never had a problem earlier and why were they allowed to reach late before. No one took the change of leadership and policies very easily. Regardless of the obstacles, the majority of students and teachers believed in the system of being disciplined and within months, all protests by parents, representations by local politicians and unwarranted interference from the police department waned. Today, I can say with pride that the school is known in the city for its discipline, academic achievement and systematic way of working. The way to transforming cultures is indeed meandering, but rewarding.

The language used for informal communication in the school, inside and outside of the classroom, was predominantly Hindi and much to my chagrin, even English language teachers conversed in Hindi. I couldn't remember any instance as a school head in the previous two decades when students conversed in their mother tongue so nonchalantly in classrooms in an English medium school. However, I made it a point to speak only in English in every setting, formal or informal—therefore, teachers had no choice but to get into the habit of doing so themselves. Teachers' unease was always writ large on their faces but fortunately, at least 75 per cent of them were comfortable speaking in English. The remaining teachers started making efforts, initially with trepidation, but after some time, willingly went all out for another non-negotiable aspect of school life.

For those who had been working in the school for the previous decade or two and were used to conversing in their home language during classroom interaction, this change became a challenge. Again, a precedence had to be set up, with a continuous exchange of ideas with them about the great import of this effort. One had to be patient but mindful of slowly moulding the school culture in the desired way. No opportunity was lost during events like the school assembly, extracurricular activities, staff development programmes and workshops to get teachers to believe in the power of impeccable expression in an English medium school. They started taking small steps and in spite of the fact that each one of them had not been turned around towards this much desired goal, the progress was enormous. Clearly, when the mission and vision get communicated and discussed throughout the school, it does make an impact on teachers and students. Posterity will decide whether I was successful in turning around the school or not. However, the rewards of appreciation started coming in from the parents who had hoped for this much desired change for a long time.

There is enough research evidence to prove that transformational principals are able to build professional learning communities (PLCs) of teachers with willing collaboration from teachers. Gradually, the learning culture starts developing organically. This further translates into an improvement in student performance. Building motivation relentlessly among teachers and students to continue to do better depends upon the morale of the entire organization. Transformational leaders have the wherewithal to turn around schools with their consistent efforts. Even the perceived or real setbacks are not constraints for such leaders. Seeing their influence as ideal, students and teachers keep building a stronger rapport with everyone, leading by example, mentoring and making ethical decisions. They not only promote teamwork but also celebrate success with their teams. They provide intellectual stimulation by asking teachers thought-provoking questions and explaining decisions. Transformational leaders are able to trust their team members to such an extent that the staff is willing to take risks for the betterment of the school. Teachers look up to them for creative solutions. No wonder then that when there are such leaders in the school, they leave a lasting impact on the thought process of all stakeholders.

Transformational leaders are effusive with their appreciation, and encouragement that gradually builds a positive organizational culture. If there is a failure to attain the commitment of teachers, this can manifest into negative behaviours in the school, which only emphasizes the role of the leader. When teachers have strong beliefs in the aims and mission of the school, they voluntarily work towards them, with a sense of responsibility and loyalty. The maxim that you can buy a person's back but you cannot buy his soul, rings most truly for transformational leadership. A sacrosanct responsibility of a transformational leader is the enhancement of individual and collective problem-solving by the leader. There is a subtle interplay between followers' needs and wants and the leader's capacity to understand these collective aspirations. The shared set of goals in the school contributes to the long-term growth of the school.

Transformational leaders create social capital in the school in such a way that it goes beyond the individual agenda. Commitment is the bedrock of such schools and every teacher buys into it. This is akin to psychologist Lev Vygotsky's concept of the 'Zone of Proximal Development', according to which a person's problem-solving process involves interaction with others and internalization of the previous experiences. Capable peers who are empathetic develop a culture of collaborative problem-solving because the sum and effectiveness of shared experiences far outweigh that of an individual. Transformative leaders utilize the shared experiences of the team to help the entire organization. These shared meanings create a high level of commitment for accomplishing organizational goals, which is why such organizations become more reflective and collaborative, strengthening their overall culture.

Moreover, in such organizations, the leader alone does not influence teachers but even teachers build stronger relationships, reducing teacher isolation. Staff development opportunities become reasons to bond with each other and reach a higher level of effectiveness. Sharing is the key here. Every day, when teachers and students come to such a school, they are sure that this will be yet another day of learning for them. They look at the leader with great optimism, since they know that they will be provided support and recognition for their efforts. They are inspired to reach for the improbable with trust-based leadership at the helm.

To sum up, transformational leadership affirms the centrality of the principal's reforming role in shaping organizational culture. The leader has to merge a personal mission of life with that of the organization to have a long-term impact and leave a valuable legacy. This is a process of self-actualization for a leader where the pursuit of a higher purpose and change for the better become the continuous focus of the school, transcending the leader's own self-interest for the sake of the organization.

# 6

# Adapting to Change and Reinventing the Organization

Flexible or adaptive leadership is especially important when there are substantial changes in a situation or when an unusual event disrupts the work and the leadership behaviour relevant to it. Differences in a situation can occur within the same position, during a transition to another position or when there are major organizational changes. Besides, a change in the political climate of the country also may have an impact on school education. An unprecedented global pandemic like Covid-19 was a complete upheaval that made all schools and leaders adapt to the continuously unfolding situation. It led to an all-encompassing change in the way education was looked at and recast educationists' view of schooling, teaching and learning forever. Teachers and leaders, along with the entire student and parent community, had to adapt to this change. In schools, leaders adapted first to get the whole organization moving towards online education, which was hitherto a less explored way of school teaching in India. New skills, competencies and behaviours were learnt by all and leaders played the most important role since people were used to a particular system which remained more or less unchanged for years, if not decades. Those who made desired choices quickly succeeded faster than those who didn't. Demands were modified and expectations shifted, new lessons learnt and technology adopted faster than it was ever done before (Fig. 6). This was manifested as crisis management in some organizations and for others, presented a perfect example of flexible leadership in such a situation.

However, in normal circumstances also, there are changing priorities with multiple objectives that are interrelated. The need to balance competing objectives or values can be daunting, to say the least. Task objectives that must be achieved have to be balanced with concern for people. This gives rise to greater autonomy to all team members as also a chance of learning from mistakes to advance forward. The trade-off between efficiency and innovative adaptation and short-term and long-term goals needs strategic management. Cognitive complexity and

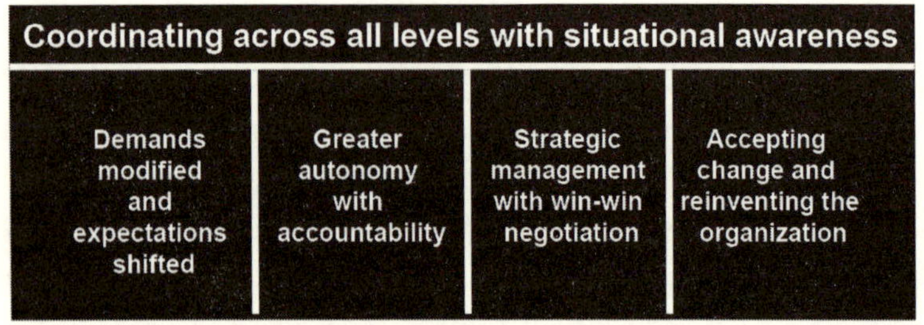


**Fig. 6: Flexible Leadership**

systems thinking include the ability to understand how the various parts of an organization relate to each other and how changes in one part of the system eventually affect the other parts. What is required here is situational awareness and social intelligence, which, in turn, requires the ability to be flexible about one's own behaviour. A leader has to have emotional intelligence, which includes the ability to recognize and regulate one's emotions and empathy for the feelings of others that are essential for determining how to influence and motivate them. Self-awareness includes the ability to understand one's own values, motives and effectiveness in influencing others.

Openness to learning and new ideas is one of the most important personality traits essential for flexible leadership. The ability to take any feedback, both positive and negative, shows the strength of leaders. This helps them learn how to improve certain patterns of behaviour which can help in achieving organizational goals. New ways of dealing with problems can only be learnt when the leader is willing to lend an ear to feedback. Sometimes, role conflicts occur when expectations of various team members do not match. To have a win-win situation, some negotiation and interpersonal influence are required. Competing values can be effectively dealt with in a highly integrated system. It is like 'tough love' that involves balancing values for human relations and task-goal achievement. Another way to put it is to term it as a 'practical vision', a vision that involves balancing values for change and stability. It means that the practices which got the organization to a particular position may not get it to the next higher position unless the leader and the team members have the capacity to be flexible.

While I was working as head of the geography department in a school which had the same leader at the helm for more than two decades, a change of leadership occurred due to the retirement of the principal. Within days, a new principal was appointed. He had been working in a boarding school, but ours was a day school, and the new leader had no clue about the requirements of such a school. He had only worked in a residential school throughout his career. He found it difficult to accept that teachers were leaving in the afternoon at the stipulated time since he wanted teachers to stay on till very late, even if there was no work. He increased the teachers' timings and all meetings started taking place late in the evening since he was used to doing this. I distinctly remember how on one occasion, all the school teachers got late after a result discussion which continued way past 8 p.m. All this caused a lot of disharmony and dissatisfaction among teachers since what they had always done well in time was getting unnecessarily delayed for no rhyme or reason. It became de rigueur for everyone to hang around the school well past evening since it was the duration of time spent in school that mattered to the principal, not the quality of work done within a set timeframe.

Clearly, the new principal tried to impose his own way of working, as practised in boarding schools, causing consternation all around. He couldn't change and adapt to the new working environment, which required a completely different way of working. Within a few months of his joining, teachers created a union and the school became a hotbed of politics. Everything that the school had ever achieved started falling by the wayside. This was a typical case of inflexibility in the leader which destroyed the educational fabric of the school. After that, there has only been a downhill journey for the school.

Social perceptiveness of a leader goes a long way in attaining the appropriate behaviour required in a particular organization. The above example shows how it was completely missing in the leader. Such leaders have to shed the baggage of past experiences and slowly mould themselves to the expectations of the organization. Of course, incremental changes can be brought in with the help of social perceptiveness. But to raze a system to rubble without having an iota of empathy for the already existing system for years on, doesn't bode well for any educational institution. The ability to self-monitor stands the leader in good stead, ensuring that he/she will be effective with flexibility.

What exactly is appropriate behaviour is a question that we can ask. A reasonable answer will be that when the leader's response is functional in being helpful to group performance by facilitating coordination, cohesion, task accomplishment and problem-solving, it is surely appropriate. Multiple expectations and the responses to them have to be juggled effectively to the satisfaction of a larger group. Contextual demands keep changing but a flexible leader will continue to skilfully execute what needs to be done. The ability to move quickly, to deal with ambiguity and to accept changes are some of the qualities of a flexible leader.

During the Covid-19 pandemic crisis and the 68 days nationwide lockdown in India in 2020, for instance, rapid technological change, new forms of socializing with virtual interaction and physical distance from people gave many opportunities to school leaders to learn flexible behaviours. However, those, who had not experienced such dire situations earlier, felt an emotional setback, which reflected on the morale of the organization. This is where leading by example remains relevant for leadership to impel sustainable and continuous improvement. Many leaders learnt a wide range of relevant behaviours, many of them undergoing training for Information Communication Technology (ICT) themselves with the rest of the team. Contrary to the earlier situation, the process of supervision and guidance changed when everyone was working from home. This needed a dexterous approach by the leader, who had to remain visible and continue to coach and mentor teachers. Objectives and priorities were repeatedly clarified; priorities and new standards were set in time and helpful feedback continued to navigate the organization through turbulent times. By appealing to teachers' values and emotions, commitment towards the organization was strengthened. Those who could take greater initiative in an uncertain environment were given more important roles while those who were less competent were encouraged to change incrementally to live up to the expectations of the organization. Resources were made available to make the organization's technical infrastructure more robust for teachers to be able to work with. At virtually every step, leaders had to reinvent themselves to stay adaptive and flexible.

I would like to give a personal example of how inflexible leadership can kill all the innovation in a school, or for that matter, in any organization. As the deputy leader of a school during my early career in school administration, I also taught geography to the senior-most class. I had always taught this practical and dynamic subject with real-life examples, as I have mentioned elsewhere in the book. However, I noticed a lot of resistance on the part of the academic coordinator who controlled the school tightly, not allowing any new ideas to be disseminated. Incidentally, she happened to be the principal's wife whose only job was to police the school. After discussing the chapter on manufacturing industries with a broad outline, I took the class for a visit to a sugar factory which was about 50 km from the school. The red tape in which time was wasted to get permission from the school was very demotivating. However, not being one to lose heart easily, I waited till the official permission was granted for the visit and then accompanied the students, happy to see how they learnt first-hand about the factors affecting sugar production. They observed the plant for themselves, talking with shop floor managers, observing the labour working there and interacting with the higher officials—in this way, the factors affecting the manufacturing process became live, real and vivid to them. The entire group returned after a very meaningful day spent there, resulting in intensive direct learning. Later, they wrote a report on various manufacturing processes along with data analysis, interviews with managers and illustrated it with photographs. However, much to my dismay, within a few days I was asked by the principal and academic coordinator to explain when I would start teaching the topic in the prescribed way! This showed a rigid mindset as she turned a blind eye to the actual learning that had already taken place.

Needless to say, the school continued to impede innovation, which resulted in a higher attrition rate of teachers since they felt impeded in their creativity. The school continued to languish in academic performance, with teachers leaving for better opportunities elsewhere. The traditional mode of teaching continued till an inquiry was conducted for the school by the educational society which ran it. Following the findings that showed the conventional, unimaginative way of functioning, the school leadership was changed by the educational society.

Clearly, providing paths to circumvent bureaucracy and red tape is a prerequisite for flexible leadership. It takes courage on the part of the school leader to be flexible. However, closed mindsets do not allow any innovation, thinking it to be a risk which they don't want to take. The types of decisions and actions needed for effective flexible leadership may not be consistent with traditional role expectations in an organization. The outmoded beliefs and irrelevant norms, such as centralized authority, highly prescriptive teaching, intolerance for any mistake, are only some of the factors that do not allow flexible or adaptive leadership. Success in adapting to changes require collective learning and collaboration by many members of the organization which need to be encouraged and facilitated by the leader. Also, the leader has to explain why change is necessary to build confidence and commitment for a new strategy or initiative. To be successful in leading change, leaders must continually assess progress, learn from experience and make necessary revisions in strategies.

To sum up, adaptability, flexibility and versatility are traits that go a long way in developing leadership effectiveness. The two key factors here are the ability to correctly diagnose a given situation for identifying an appropriate behaviour response and second, the ability to perform that behaviour effectively. Together, they can facilitate coordination, cohesion, task accomplishment and problem-solving, thus bringing in effective learning outcomes for students. The four primary perspectives for flexible leadership are human relations, open systems, internal processes and rational role models. Instead of using the top-down approach to the leader's use of power and self-assertion, flexible leadership builds high expectations and accountability with a supportive orientation in the school. It promotes collective intelligence in the system, which should be the goal for each educational institution.

# 7

# When People Say, We Do It

Stories of leadership successes follow a familiar structure. A charismatic leader takes over a struggling school, establishes new goals and expectations and challenges the 'business as usual' perspective within the organization. This leader then creates new organizational routines and structures that over time transform the school culture, contributing in turn to greater teacher satisfaction, higher teacher expectations for students and improved student achievement. The number of administrative tasks a principal undertakes typically leaves insufficient hours in the day to complete not only the 'heroic' activities but also to cope with mundane responsibilities. Most problematic is the fact that when a heroic leader moves on, progress often comes to a standstill and previous practices re-emerge. Clearly, no leader can single-handedly lead schools to greatness since the process of leadership involves an array of individuals, all equipped with different tools and techniques.

School leadership cannot just be equated with the school principal alone. It has often been seen that the 'heroics of leadership' genre still exists, a concept which only dwells on the 'what' of leadership—the structures, functions, routines and roles of the school—rather than the 'how' of leadership, which is all about the daily performance of leadership routines. It would be a worthwhile exercise to identify what it means to take a perspective on distributed school leadership. For this, the daily interactions in a school are critical to understanding the practice of distributed leadership.

Around a decade and a half ago, distributed leadership was described as the 'new kid on the block' by author and Emeritus Professor at Monash University, Peter Gronn. Like any other new idea, it was both enthusiastically greeted by some, while summarily dismissed by others as another fad. However, distributed leadership continues to be an influential idea within educational circles. The distributed leadership concept came as a more achievable and sustainable conceptualization of leadership, replacing the model of a single 'heroic' leader standing atop a hierarchy, bending the school community to follow his or her own purpose. It involves multiple leaders, with different ways of thinking about the practice of school leadership. It distributes the responsibilities of leadership over an interactive web of people and situations, where role complementarities gain importance (Fig. 7). Decisions about who leads and who follows are determined by the task or problem situation, not by the formal position or pecking order. It then gets stretched over a number of people in different roles. Thus, it is more about the practice of leadership rather than

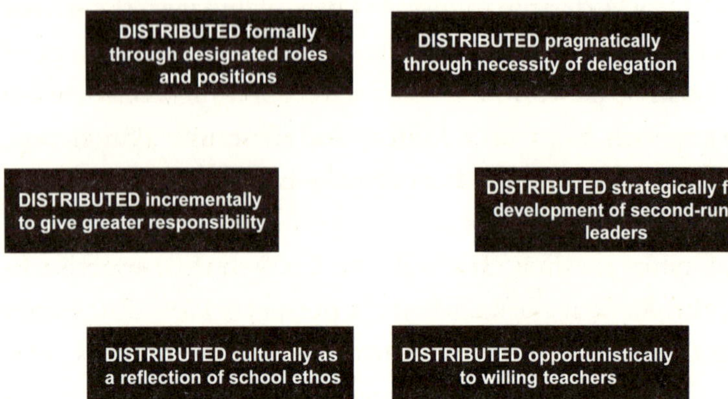


**Fig. 7: Distributed Leadership**

focusing on an individual leader. Given the close conceptual links between distributed leadership and longstanding organization phenomena as power, influence, coordination, collective decision-making and delegated authority, a key question to the proponents of distributed leadership is what this idea stands for. How does it add any value to our understanding of the phenomena of leadership?

On the credit side, distributed leadership has helped to expose inherent limitations of leadership understood as an individual's influence, but on the debit side, it has deflated the larger-than-life persona of a leader. The practice of distributed leadership typically involves multiple leaders, some with or without any formal leadership position. It is essential, therefore, to move beyond viewing leadership in terms of superhuman actions. What is of importance here is the interactions of individuals in schools. Some routines such as monitoring and evaluating teaching practices involve fewer leaders, mostly the principal and vice principal, compared with curriculum transaction and teacher development where many teachers are involved. At times, their interactions may overlap with each other. The principal emphasizes goals and standards, keeps the meetings moving, and summarizes discussions towards a logical and desirable conclusion, besides reminding teachers about what is expected of them in their classrooms.

One of the first efforts in the USA to deliberately take on the challenge of building distributed leadership capacity was the Annenberg Distributed Leadership Project (DLP). Philadelphia was the first site for this project when it began in 2004. Among the largest school districts, Philadelphia was identified as one of the most socioeconomically, financially and academically weak school districts in the country. The vision for this project involved redefining and reshaping the role of school leadership in overburdened and complex urban schools. It was envisaged with the idea of giving new dimensions to the momentum and efforts to redefine leadership in the Philadelphia School District where many schools were in the 'School Improvement' or 'Corrective Action' category due to failure to make adequate progress under the No Child Left Behind Legislation. The aim of this five-year project was to operationalize a distributed perspective on leadership in 16 schools of the city. The project targeted new school leaders and their teachers to build distributed leadership teams. It started with five goals:

- *First*, wanting to develop a model of distributed leadership.
- *Second*, planning a targeted professional development strategy for teachers.

- *Third*, aiming at developing over 80 effective teacher leaders who could then support 16 new principals.
- *Fourth*, achieving improved instructional focus and student outcomes.
- *Finally*, starting a programme of sustained leadership development.

Thus, the overarching objective of the project was to develop a distributed mindset for principals in their work, culminating in a positive impact on leadership and capacity building for the whole school growth. As a result of the project, the academic achievement grew by leaps and bounds and professional learning communities started developing. Strong evidence emerged in terms of effective team functioning, leaders' sense of self-efficacy, trust levels among team members and the principal, perceptions of school influence in the community and teacher satisfaction. Professional learning communities of teachers started developing with many teachers getting training as master trainers. Teacher leaders started using data analysis for formulating school improvement strategies. In each one of the schools targeted, distributed leadership teams developed which achieved not only an improved instructional focus but also higher student outcomes. A new generation of leaders in Philadelphia emerged who were well-grounded in the skills and strategies needed to sustain high-performing, standards-based schools. In summary, the DLP provided an effective example of lasting school-level changes.

There are enough anecdotal evidences of this model from various schools. One of the recent examples from my last school pertains to the exhaustive work done for the annual survey conducted by an educational journal. Every year, this work goes to the librarian who collates data from various departments and sends this to the journal. However, this year, owing to her being unavailable due to a medical issue at home, this work was spontaneously taken over by the school counsellor. She had never done it before but she learnt how to do it systematically. She collected information from various departments and answered the survey. The exhaustive survey was accomplished to the maximum satisfaction of the school. Whenever we had a need for other people to step in for some urgent work, it just happened without being 'instructed' by the principal, even if teachers have to burn their midnight oil or learn new tasks from scratch. They did not have to wait for the principal to come into the picture since the levels of relational trust were high in the school. The school didn't come to a standstill during the absence of the principal or other office-bearers since the work culture prevailed on its own—the teachers knew that the principal will stand by their decisions. However, there are schools where most urgent and important decisions are also stalled when the principal is not there. Clearly, no one else is trusted in the school and leadership is tightly vested in just one person, a case of high centralization and low trust. There are not only spontaneous collaborations in the school but also intuitive working relationships which revolve around institutionalized practices.

In one of the schools where I started developing my own concept of leadership after 12 years of working in the capacity of the head of a department, leadership was well distributed among senior teachers. The question for me to ponder on was: why had the previous school which I had worked in, never developed this model? However, I was better placed to answer this question only after joining my new school. The previous school had insecure leadership as the principal did not trust anyone and believed in having unlimited and unaccounted for powers. This led to numerous struggles by vested interests. I realized that the school was caught in a time warp, even after more than two decades of leaving it—frozen in time. It never had a leader who could create any momentum in the school. All that was ever done day after day, week after week and month after month, now adding to decades, was routine work. Teaching in the lecture mode was the practice. Activities outside the textbook were looked upon as a waste of time, attendance of teachers considered of more importance than competence, and technologically, the school was a laggard.

If one visits the current principal's office, there is pin-drop silence—the unsaid rule in the school. Interactions do not happen—teachers meet the principal only when they absolutely need to, and that too with a prior appointment, and after a communication is sent to teachers with a handwritten note in the register. Secrecy is the most important dictum in every school function. When one visits that school, it seems like a classic scene from Charles Dickens' novel, *Great Expectations*, in which Miss Havisham is stuck in time warp with cobwebs hanging in the room and a clock that has stopped. Though, the similarity in this analogy for the school ends here, yet you could be in a time machine in such a school where educational dynamism was never heard of.

In the other school I began working in, for every important action in the school, there was delegation of responsibilities among teachers who worked together on a shared basis. Each departmental head not only looked at the performance of all teachers within the department but also became a part of interdepartmental collaboration on school activities. There was not only reciprocity among teachers in the school but also a collective sense of responsibility. The principal observed the classes very sparingly but motivated the departmental heads to monitor the performance of each teacher. For the first time in my life, I sat with the principal, chairperson and board members of the school on the interview board, where I was requested to interview every candidate thoroughly for subject knowledge. Till then, I was only aware that for subject expertise, professors from universities were called, who, in my opinion had very little understanding of how schools work and what transpires in a classroom. But this school gave a lot of credibility to talent and competence of experienced teachers, making them buy into the school leader's vision. It gave me a greater sense of accountability and responsibility, since a team of teachers looked up to me for guidance and suggestions.

Our interactions pertaining to subject enrichment and student achievement often transcended the school time, bringing in a greater cohesion among the group. We compiled our resources and strategies that enabled us to address all possible problems in classroom transactions. We knew that we were trusted by the principal and willingly shared his vision for the school. Without doubt, this was the beginning of my lessons in leadership, which got further honed and formalized when the school also gave me myriad opportunities to lead other schools. It would be worthwhile to add that this school continues to create leaders who go on to head various schools.

This practice emerged in the school as a product of everyday interactions with various team members of the school. Situation and context also played a very important role in the practice of distributed leadership. Multiple leaders of the school may not necessarily have had a formal position, nor did the school have any given type or number of followers. Each organizational function created numerous leadership roles and it was during the team members' interactions that the distributed leadership emerged, as it often happens in most schools where this leadership model is practised. At times, some of these actions may overlap with each other since there is always a reciprocal interdependency between these leaders. After class observations, engaging teachers with feedback gives the principal and the vice principal a situational setting to reiterate the goals and expectations of the school. There could be spontaneous collaboration among people or institutionalized practices for distributing leadership.

Distributed leadership has normative power since it reflects current changes in leadership practices around the world. Leadership gets actively and purposefully distributed within the school among various people. This requires crossing multiple types of boundaries across which ideas and insights are shared, traversing even a very different organizational landscape. It makes a positive difference to organizational outcomes and student learning by incorporating multiple groups of individuals in a school who work at guiding and mobilizing staff in the instructional change process. More pertinent questions to be asked are how leadership is distributed and what impact it is having on school improvement. Distributed leadership is considered by some educators as a cure-all for all ailments of the school, an opinion which is far-fetched. It should instead be viewed as a conceptual or diagnostic tool that can be enriched with the help of systematic evidence.

However, distributing leadership among too many people can sometimes be problematic since it may result in greater incompetence. It is only desirable when the quality of actions and activities contribute to assisting teachers to provide more effective instruction to students. Individual characteristics and behaviours, the standards people live up to, and the influence they exert on their followers are some of the features that need to be considered while distributing leadership. That doesn't also mean that we become blinkered to the limitations of the concept itself or our ability to think about it. However, it is neither a panacea nor a blueprint, but a way of getting under the skin of leadership practice and illuminating the possibilities for organizational transformation.

# 8

# Continuous Reinvention and Creativity

We are at a threshold when societies and cultures are being reformed. We know that the way life used to exist once or the way we thought it should, doesn't work any longer. A leadership mindset for the future with a new view of the world is needed to address the complexities and challenges of the 21st century skills. Albert Einstein had famously said that we cannot address the problems of today with the same mindset that created those problems. An enquiring mindset which takes initiatives with innovation is required to thrive in the present scenario. That most of us live within the same mindset which has been prevailing for long, if not forever, is a given. It comprises our own beliefs, feelings, values and attitudes, which guide our decisions, behaviour and actions in the world. It is precisely this deep-seated mindset which can either open or close the possibilities in our personal and professional life. Thomas Kuhn, American professor and philosopher of science, whose book *The Structure of Scientific Revolutions* was published in 1962, popularized the word 'paradigm'. It is the complete pattern of thought on which a particular world view rests. Resistance to change is a natural process of the mind which does not allow us to go beyond our current understanding. Since human beings crave for stability, equilibrium and the status quo, it remains difficult to discard prevailing mindsets. This is where leadership comes in, as a social process of assessing the interplay of cultural factors which have problems of adaptation to and interaction with new mores. In fact, culture and leadership are two sides of the same coin. Leaders first create the organizational culture and then create the organizational structure.

Organizational leaders realize that they need to innovate and create every day to achieve new learning for which they have to support experimentation and risk-taking. New patterns will only emerge when we will let go of our established ways of working—this is a precursor for developing a more liberal and expanded view. It will definitely upset fixed minds that are accustomed to a certain way of working, causing discomfort. The culture of overconfidence about a system and always 'being right' is a direct threat to the development of a culture of inquiry.

A precondition required for innovative leadership is a strong willingness to engage differently with one another at work. Taking responsibility for one's own learning would foster innovation and creativity in an organization. This builds the practice of adaptation among organizational members. To build a multifaceted organization that meets the needs of today while preparing us for the future, creativity and innovation with a new mindset are a must. Barack Obama in his inaugural address of 2013 had said that we must act, knowing that our work will be imperfect. Assuming that any new idea will not work is only a deterrent and challenge. How do we then build the skills, competencies and consciousness necessary for changing the school paradigm?

In order to achieve these, innovative leaders need a powerful imagination and excellent communication skills. They are not micromanagers but focus on the big picture. Eloquent on translating the organizational vision for the whole team to generate enthusiasm, their focus is all about developing a culture of innovation rather than just getting a few creative outliers on board (Fig. 8). They are intuitive

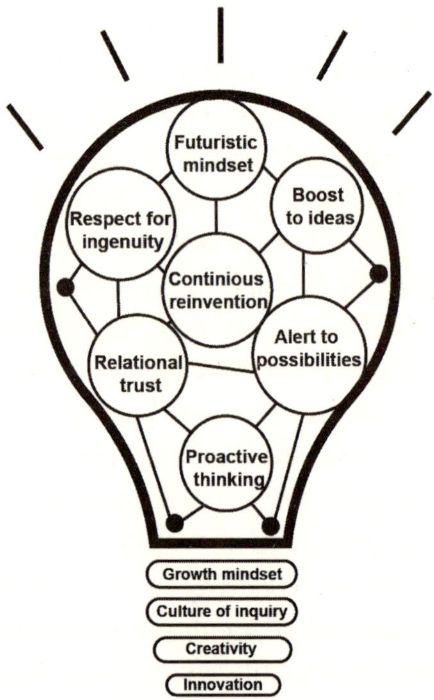


**Fig. 8: Innovative Leadership**

and always looking at the future, rather than sitting on past laurels, looking for precedents. They explore multiple opportunities and options and believe that ambiguity can be an advantage, not a problem, for that leads to finding out options. Instead of labelling ideas right or wrong, they look for 'better' ways. Their ability to look more deeply at any situation, perceiving details and seeing new patterns, make them adept at tapping into the already existing potential in the organization besides bringing in a fresh perspective. The insights thus generated, fuel innovation. They use storytelling to describe ideas, constructing future imagery by communicating effectively and using metaphors and analogies in their stories to coordinate and disseminate an idea.

Free exploration, improvisation and experimentation usher in a culture of inquiry. The focus remains on asking searching questions with critical thinking, without always expecting immediate answers. American writer Scott Fitzgerald once said that the test of a first-rate intelligence is the ability to hold two opposing ideas in the mind at the same time and still retain the ability to function effectively. Innovators shed 'either/or' thinking and live with paradoxes and contradictions to ultimately analyse, synthesize and integrate the best practices.

Rewards and recognition foster mechanisms for developing a culture of free flow of ideas. For that, leaders also must remove impediments in the way of innovative culture such as petty group dynamics, harsh criticism of new ideas, avoidance of risks and overemphasis on status quo—all of which crush ingenuity. Everyone has ideas but only some people know how to keep their 'idea factories' fortified to churn out rich innovation. As I have mentioned elsewhere, the cause of sustainability is very close to my heart. However, there are stark contrasts in how these ideas were taken by the senior management of the school. In one school, I received a national award for my efforts in reviving water resources with community collaboration and the work of students. On the other hand, in the school where I was working till recently, the idea of bringing in sustainability processes was crushed nonchalantly.

When I noticed that every year students buy their books and stationery from the school bookshop which packs them in big plastic bags, I put forth the idea of jute bags. This bag, if well designed, could also be reused repeatedly for shopping purposes by the family. I especially got the bag designed with the school logo and its vision written on it. The bag was sent for approval to the senior management which delegated the matter further, asking the director of administration to look into it. He rejected the idea outright on some pretext, saying that it could not be done since a change in existing practices was not acceptable. It was obvious that he didn't want to ruffle any feathers or perhaps he had some vested interest in letting the stationer use plastic bags. I never got to know the reason but the idea was killed even before it could be considered on its merit, leave alone implemented. The school still continues with the same bags, and I have learnt the harder way that every management doesn't value innovative ideas. Maintaining the status quo brings comfort in some people's lives and they do not want any change in what is going on for years. Clearly, such schools have no fluidity in accepting ideas.

Yet, there are schools which promote innovation. They nurture creative people and provide them with required resources and space to experiment, always encouraging mind mapping in meetings and practising brainstorming with team members. Even though they recognize that extreme pressure of the workload, unrealistic in expectations, can also hamper creativity, they also know that challenging work is conducive for innovation. Setting up space, both literally and metaphorically, for ingenious people to encourage interaction among people is a great booster to creativity.

Innovation is more likely when people from different disciplines, backgrounds and areas of expertise share their thinking. Diversity brings diverse ideas on the table. Many researches have proved that a higher level of 'identity integration' displays higher levels of creativity when problems require drawing on different realms of knowledge. For example, the Wright brothers who conceptualized and flew the world's first motor-operated airplane were motivated to invent aviation because they romanced with the technical challenges and the quest for human flight.

One such leader who was like an 'idea factory' was the chairman of a school I worked in. He could change the entire culture of the organization with his expertise in storytelling. He established a school in a city which only had traditional schooling. where teachers taught in the same way they had for years, where parents expected continuity in the education system without any change and the principals believed that they already knew everything. However, the school chairman was a person with numerous ideas, some challenging the set way of thinking and some sounding so outlandish initially that they weren't easily accepted by people at first.

He entrusted new responsibilities to the principal instead of following the usual rigmarole of administration. The responsibilities included holding educational symposiums for teachers and getting experts from all walks of life to participate in them. Teachers were encouraged to think beyond the box and gradually exhorted to develop a reading culture, in a system where reading beyond textbooks was never imagined. Not only did he ensure that the best of educational journals and magazines were subscribed to, but he also sat through the various reading and discussion sessions himself, lending credibility to his efforts. He started by telling stories and swayed the general thinking that stayed limited only to the immediate lives and environment.

Awards were constituted for the most thoughtful questions made for test papers by teachers which made them explore their subject and topics with critical and creative thinking. Students were told to meet with him and tell him about any ideas which they wanted materialized. If they were found promising, seed money was given to them to develop them into tangible products and services. Within a couple of years, the entire school was found turning to innovation since it not only gave satisfaction to the stakeholders involved but also led to a feeling of immense achievement. Clearly, a lot can be achieved by leaders who can move all the stakeholders for realizing their ideas and dreams.

Reaching a mastery of innovative leadership starts with leaders themselves. They have a strong sense of who they are from inside out. They are always aware of their mode of thinking in a given moment, whether defeatist, dreamy, sustaining, stabilizing or innovating—sometimes all rolled into one. They know how and when to shift the mindset, bringing in a lot of energy as they play the balanced role of both a participant as well as an observer in the work they are doing. Knowing their own strengths, weaknesses and also recognizing blind spots is a good starting point for innovative leaders as the ability to manage the ego, boosting humility and enabling true empathy reduces defensiveness and the tendency to take things personally. They refrain from judging prematurely since that kills ideas in a discussion and affects decision-making.

One of the organizations I worked with was an educational start-up. It had only a few people in the team when I joined as executive director. The organization already had a director with whom I had to work. Both of us came from the school leadership background, though I had more experience of working in many schools and leading for more (number of) years. However, I was happy to work with another person who was senior to me by the appointment date. Within weeks, I noticed that all my enthusiasm for work was diminished since the existing director clearly felt threatened by me. Ironically, that feeling of insecurity was manifested in belittling me publicly and privately. I could hardly ever give my opinion on anything earlier since the previous director was the sole in charge of academics. Now, she was unwilling to share any responsibility with me. I could have ignored it, doing what was required of me till it became obvious to the whole team that I was not only being sidelined but also slighted.

Arrogance indeed is the camouflage of insecurity. The team members asked me if I would continue to let myself be treated this way. No prize for guessing that I left the organization within a year since it was clear that talent was not respected there. The discriminatory attitude of the CEO made it easier for me to leave the organization. When what matters is only seniority, then there's no reason to expect any contribution by new talent. Today, that educational organization is in a shambles and no one who is competent stays there for long.

Having always been a keen environmentalist, as already mentioned in the example of introducing the jute bag, I brought in the idea in a school that all students and teachers should refrain from using aluminium foil to pack their lunch, since it is a non-renewable resource. Instead, everyone must think about better and eco-friendly alternatives. Slowly, the amount of aluminium foil used in the school got reduced, but many teachers and parents complained that the shift from foil paper to cloth napkins leads to greater use of detergent and water, which, in turn, adds to the environmental cost. We discussed this with various people who had done enough research on the issue and after comparative cost-benefit analysis, it was found that the original way of packing food was much better. Instead of taking it personally as an offence to my sense of self, I encouraged the school to revoke the previous idea. Also, I went ahead to find out where the used aluminium foil could be sent for recycling purposes.

The Students' Council formed a committee for collecting all used foil paper safely and to send it every month for recycling. It is a clear example of how some leaders can go beyond their own egos and use every challenge to turn into an opportunity for new innovations. Incidentally, this was one of the first schools in the entire state where handmade paper was made by students by recycling the used paper, following the maxim of 'Reduce, Recycle and Reuse'.

Later, this school would go on to win a national award for environmental management, as mentioned in one of the chapters.

Innovative leaders continue to reinvent themselves, training their sights on their own growth and development at all times, never convinced that they know everything already. Leaning too much on a smug satisfaction of how much knowledge one has can make one complacent. Nor should one be perpetually dissatisfied with oneself for that would lead to a crippling impact. Neither extreme is good for innovation. These leaders know how to navigate the organization through thick and thin, motivating team members to think for themselves by posing questions instead of handing out readymade answers. Even when they know the answer, they let team members think independently to hone their own skills and learn from their mistakes. They continually check and question any well-thought-out plan against emerging information to ensure that it still fits the specific situation, and they always make their assumptions explicit.

To achieve this level of innovativeness, leaders have to ensure psychological safety so that a culture of relational trust builds in the organization. Making breakthroughs requires the assurance that even if someone fails at an idea, it will not be held against him. For this they need to make enough room for vulnerability. They neither avoid conflicts nor seek them; rather, they deal with them comfortably. As the story of recycling aluminium foil suggests, the school saw that the person at the helm could also explore an idea even when it might or might not succeed and it became a lesson in as well as a reason for innovation to everyone. They learnt that regardless of the success or failure of an idea, the key is to keep innovating. It is not surprising, therefore, that such schools continue to remain high on motivation since they look at ideas as opportunities, not threats. How wonderful it is that schools like these do not feel dated!

Rapid flow of information is very necessary in such an organization. Innovative leaders keep the feedback loop small to avoid wastage of time, tapping ideas from all ranks, instead of focusing too much on hierarchy for innovative decisions. Innovative leaders allow people to pursue their passions and set some time apart for them in the regular schedule, recognizing that passionate engagement in one's work is highest when the work is looked up to as a noble responsibility. Can anything be nobler than working for the cause of education, combining research with practice, which shapes the future of civilization?

After reaching the desired level of success, many innovative leaders grow more conservative with experimentation, fearing they might lose all the success they have achieved so assiduously. However, continual renewing and reinventing will keep not only the organization forever new but also the leader forever innovative.

Information and Communication Technology (ICT) in Indian schools during the turn of this century was neither commonplace nor widely accepted. All documentation work in schools were done on paper, registers were made for entries of examination marks, and emails were used very sparingly. Mr Sanjiv Kumar was one of the most innovative leaders at the helm of the management of four Delhi Public Schools. I was leading one of his schools which was in a city in Punjab. Progress in the field of ICT advanced so rapidly that within a few years, the school became a leading light of technical and academic innovations in the state. All communication in the school was shifted on email, both through the intranet and internet. Teachers communicated to parents and the school leader sent all official messages to teachers only through emails. Students took up international projects by connecting to their peers from across the globe, bringing in global accolades from even the United Nations Environment Programme (UNEP).

Gradually, the school became almost paperless with the entire administrative work shifting online. At a time when school admissions were conducted in person, all applications for student admission and teacher recruitment were carried out online. Initially, there was an uproar among parents who were opposed to the idea of depositing school fees in the online mode, but it was just a matter of time for them to discover that it was time-saving and error-free for everyone concerned. Teachers could generate student progress cards through software, the librarian could keep stock of thousands of books easily and also assess which books were most widely read by students and teachers, which led to the annual book buying process becoming easier. It was clear what genres of books were more popular and what interests could be inculcated further for developing a reading culture. It was helpful to see which characters, authors and genres were more prominently read, all with the introduction of information technology.

Parents got regular communication about the home assignments set for the day, while the principal got all discipline and academic reports of the large school with just a click. These were only some of the ways that changed the way people worked. Technology and its early adoption catalysed the entire process of schooling by making it more efficient and effective.

Clearly, innovative leaders continuously embrace the mode of thinking that grasps opportunity, passionately alert to the possibilities thrown by the power of imagination and to the thrill of turning vision into reality. While others may see challenges and impediments, they find potential, which gives rise to a fresh perspective and attitude. They just keep pressing ahead, sure that progress will happen. They are adept at assaulting assumptions because the brain left to its own devices routinely takes what brain researchers call 'perceptual shortcuts' to save time and energy.

Years of experience in the field can sometimes be a setback for people if they don't continually innovate, fixed in the position that 'It's always done this way' or 'We have tried this, but it doesn't work', even without giving an opportunity to themselves to try fresh ideas or for that matter the other people's ideas. Isn't it more creative to ask, 'What would an entirely different way of handling this situation look like?' As can be seen through the example of the executive director mentioned earlier, when a leader starts imagining that he or she knows what is to be done in which way, without keeping any room for change, then it is the beginning of the end of an organization. Hubris and innovation are incompatible. It is, therefore, not a surprise that the said organization is on its last legs.

The moment a fresh idea comes to their awareness, innovative leaders are open to experiment with alternatives and possibilities. They step outside of their culture bubble and interact with more people to wrap their brain gently around the ideas they are trying to express, thinking proactively ahead of the curve of a situation. Realizing that things often happen like a flashlight when a person is not paying much attention, they know that responding to even issues in their own personal lives, along with societal, technological and other external changes can generate new ideas and trends. By assessing and interpreting changes as they relate to the world of work, they position themselves to transform them into new opportunities to build empowering environments.

# 9

# Achieving a Common Goal with Synergy

The 21st century has been littered with divisiveness, partisanship and aggressiveness. The options then left to us are isolation versus bridge building and polarized encampments versus collaboration for synergy. A common question asked is, who indeed is a collaborative leader? The answer is simple: Irrespective of the role one plays in a school, one can become a collaborative leader once one has chosen to invest oneself in the improvement of the school. How does a collaborative relationship build up? It is when there is mutual respect between the leader and teachers involved in the collaboration, transcending self-interest. When the goals of people merge, the ensuing relationship gets collaborative. It is a highly purposeful exercise of behaviour, communication and organizational resources that affect the perspective and belief of another person. It is a very skilful job and needs organizing, managing, leading and sustaining that symbiotic association of team members in the school.

Schools offer numerous opportunities for teachers and the principal, and teachers and students to collaborate on projects and activities. Sometimes teachers are unwilling to collaborate, particularly when they could be doing far better than the others in achieving their learning goals. It may even be due to inertia on their part. Collaboration requires extending oneself beyond the regular comfort zone since it takes a team of workers and the interplay among them to reach the required goal. A collaborative leader could, however, make the process easier by looking for opportunities where more people can come together for a desired outcome. Partnering with a team member leads to collaboration and the exchange of ideas for best practices.

When I joined my first school in 1985, within two years, the school started the celebration of its fiftieth year. One of the ideas given by the school chairman was to organize a photographic exhibition, charting its long legacy and the richness of its educational journey. A team was constituted, but to everyone it looked like a most disparate team since none of the members had ever worked together. I was one of the team members and along with me there was a Hindi teacher who drew like an artist and a very outgoing teacher who excelled in connecting with people, using her brilliant interpersonal skills. Since this school was well-established, with many senior teachers who were highly sceptical about the new teachers, this group was already written off by everyone.

Not to be deterred, we set out for our task most diligently. The teacher, who was good at networking, started meeting many people, such as former teachers, school alumni and dignitaries who had graced numerous occasions in the school and could help us to find interesting photographs. The school archives were in an utter state of neglect but she managed to find memorable photographs there. The Hindi teacher, who drew very well and was an expert in calligraphy, started making artistic labels for photographs which were beautifully mounted on ivory sheets. The sepia toned photos on ivory paper, handwritten labels, mostly poetic in Hindi and English, added to the allure of the pictures. I was good at making creative titles using poetry and extracts from classic prose. We were all given a month and a room to finish the task and we did so—in spite of facing a lot of ridicule by senior teachers.

Finally, when that exhibition emerged from the room to a large hall, everyone was awestruck. No one could believe such an exhibition could be put up by school teachers, since the whole ambience of the hall turned into an art gallery. Clearly, the chairman was a person who saw the potential in teachers and believed in our competence. We collaborated with each other, strengthening our expertise and synergizing our efforts, finally producing an excellent exhibition that was appreciated by thousands of people who visited it during the next few months. Alone we could have done so little, but together we translated the school vision and mission into an exhibition.

Many leaders look at their teams with greater reflection, opening their minds to appreciate everyone's good practices. It is also referred to as 'strolling for moving schools' and encouraging collaborative decision-making. The principal's leadership here sets the tone for professional reflection and collaboration based on a learning-oriented approach for the school.

As a newly appointed teacher for geography in a school in Delhi, I was given a fortnight to join. I had just earned my BEd degree and was waiting to join the school on the said date. The school had already started after the summer vacation but the new teachers were expected to join after a week. To my surprise, I was called by the school one day to meet with the vice principal, who was also heading the department of geography. On reaching the school, I went to his office but couldn't find him there. On enquiring from the front office, I was told to either wait indefinitely for hours or go and look for him in the school building. I preferred the latter option but had never met him before and, therefore, would not have recognized him. I was amused when I was told by the receptionist that I could never miss him because wherever there was a group of teachers surrounding a person in the corridor or a cohort of students interacting animatedly with someone outside a class, I would find him. This description seemed most bizarre to me but it wasn't just said in jest.

I set forth as directed, to locate him and within minutes, I came across a crowd of teachers outside the staffroom, laughing and chatting happily with a person of nondescript appearance but a strong magnetic quality. Everyone around him was looking buoyant and delighted. When they saw a stranger approaching them, they asked me who I was looking for. As I told them I wanted to meet the vice principal, one of the teachers said, 'So, you are the new geography teacher. Tighten your belt to get ready to take seat in the spaceship.' The vice principal added to this banter by saying, 'Welcome on board,' and then excitedly introduced me to all the teachers. From there began a wonderful journey of 12 years under a most endearing guide and mentor.

Needless to say, the entire school revolved around the vice principal and everyone was forever eager to collaborate with him on any task given. He could get anyone on board to work collectively and untiringly on a task, with total commitment.

Collaborative leadership, thus, emphasizes structures and processes that foster a shared commitment to achieving school improvement goals. The practice involves developing a shared vision for change and then enabling people to work collaboratively to achieve that vision (Fig. 9). Increasing the school's capacity for improvement represents a key target of strategic leadership efforts designed to affect teacher practice and student learning. Providing the means

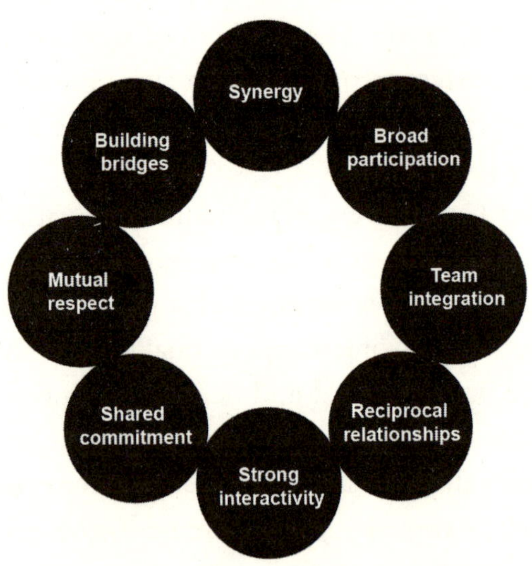


**Fig. 9: Collaborative Leadership**

for implementing strategic action aimed at continuous improvement and tapping into this process can be achieved through collaboration in the school. In this way, teachers develop a dynamic view of school improvement by expanding the school's academic capacity through this process.

There are many reciprocal-effect relationships that exist in a school which have feedback loops running across the group of teachers. When the school has a culture of freely expressing its feedback on the teaching and learning process, it exerts a positive impact on student outcomes. After observing teachers' classes, I prefer to give them the feedback soon after, which helps them to connect to their own pedagogical practice. Delayed feedback has little or no relevance. The teacher stays back after school to have coffee with me to discuss the class methodology in detail. I also enquire about their well-being and family in the course of this discussion, which makes the principal-teacher bond stronger. Even if a negative feedback is to be given, it remains constructive in such an environment and the teacher leaves with a greater awareness about her teaching and a deeper commitment towards the school.

A learning-oriented approach in the school brings about its all-round development. Professional reflection on practice and collaborative work supports a culture of mutual learning. Conflict among peers gets replaced by collaborative practices instead of peer competition. Also called 'co-leadership', members in a collaborative school participate more readily in learning with each other to reach the common goal.

Formal positions in a school are often given to the vice principal, headmistress and academic coordinators. A principal, who works well with them by relating to them, transcends the psychological dynamics in leadership. Leadership is not solely concerned with the rational side of organizational life but also with the emotions that drive group and organization dynamics. Clearly, such a leader has a boundary-keeping function which fosters institutional functioning effectively. Far from diluting the influence of the leader in the central role, it offers a singularly inspiring vision to all the stakeholders. It is not just delegation of roles and responsibilities but also the leadership team integrating across the organization. Differences of opinion, conflicts of interest and underlying tensions are an inherent part of an organizational life, causing stress and anxiety, but it is the personal presence of the top leadership that can lead to collaborative solutions.

A longitudinal study of school improvement was conducted in 192 elementary schools in an American state in 2010. The study employed annual surveys of teachers and parents as means of understanding patterns of change in the strength of collaborative leadership and academic capacity in these schools over a four-year period. These perceptions were then compared with the growth in the reading achievement of a cohort of more than 12,000 elementary school students as they moved from Grade 3 through to Grade 5. The survey items were designed to reflect three specific aspects of collaborative leadership within each school:

1. Making collaborative decisions focusing on educational improvement.
2. Emphasizing school governance that empowers staff and students, encouraging commitment, broad

participation and shared accountability for student learning.

3. Emphasizing participation in efforts to evaluate the school's academic development.

The data analysis done through factor means showed that schools made considerable growth in reading over time, which led to a substantial enhancement of student learning (approximately 50 per cent). Thus, the study provides empirical support for the proposition that collaborative leadership positively impacts the student learning by building the academic capacity of schools. Further, the study takes note of sources of school leadership beyond the principal and explicitly links a more team-oriented and collaborative approach to school leadership with capacity building strategies designed to impact teaching and learning.

Proponents of collaborative leadership also suggest that it has the potential to account for naturally occurring leadership processes that exist in schools beyond the formal leadership exercised by principals. Acknowledging and developing the broader leadership capacity in schools may hold the key to unlocking the store of leadership potential grounded in instructional expertise that principals are often unable to provide with their numerous administrative duties. Building and sustaining professional learning communities is easier in collaborative schools. With myriad strings of interaction among teachers, enduring bonds and relationships are made. The sensitivity of the principal in such systems cannot be overemphasized since constructively engaging diverse groups of teachers poses great challenges, besides adding great value. A team with different experiences, knowledge and perspectives can make more creative and informed decisions, but what is needed on the leader's part is to build social capital to sustain this diverse community.

Leadership is not a prerogative of only a privileged few—it can come from all walks of society. People feel most comfortable within their own 'tribe' as the cliché goes. However, since the world of work often operates across the tribal lines, collaboration doesn't come naturally to everyone. What is required of the collaborative leader is the integration of these strong groups through motivation and the school structure. Once the ties are built, they only get stronger with the influence of collaborative leaders. Bridges of trust running across teams can hold everyone together in the common goal of school improvement.

# 10

# Empowering Teachers to Build More Leaders

Globalization is the order of the day, leading to a new global economy that depends on the production, application and dissemination of knowledge. This is the reason why human capital is central to this new world order. Schools also accommodate themselves to the changing realities to keep pace with the way people work and communicate. The concept of teachers' leadership has become increasingly embedded in the practice of educational improvement, its central tenet being that teachers hold an important position in the operation of schools. As active involvement by all individuals within the various domains of an organization gains currency, the idea of teacher leadership keeps getting more realistic. Today's schools are too complex for principals to lead alone and hierarchical bureaucracies are being challenged across the board, just as it is in other global spaces. Each teacher's perspective can inform the

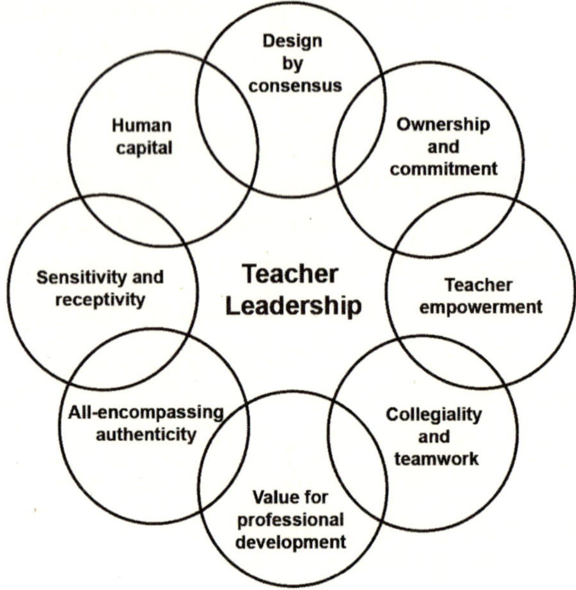


**Fig. 10: Teacher Leadership**

management of the school and result in effective decisions. Greater teacher participation leads to greater ownership and commitment to the school goals (Fig. 10). Since they have participated in making decisions, with their perspectives taken cognisance of, they are more likely to see that these decisions get implemented—this gives them a feeling of empowerment. American educationist Roland S. Barth (2001) famously said that the teacher who leads, gets to sit at the table with grown-ups as a first class citizen in the school rather than as a subordinate in a world full of subordinates. 'Teachers who assume responsibility for something they care desperately about…stand at the gate of profound learning' (Barth 2001, p. 445).

Teachers are the ones who have frontline knowledge of classroom issues, which lay the foundation of their work, and teacher interactions break through teacher isolation, creating a more professional work environment. Collegiality certainly promotes organizational integration and its journey towards excellence. The real beneficiaries are students when they see adults practise participatory forms of communication. Teachers become leaders when they function in professional learning communities to affect student learning, thereby contributing to school improvement. A long-term enhanced sense of community life starts taking shape in the school. Their leadership encompasses interrelated domains of commitment and knowledge, including the moral purpose of all education. Teacher leadership aligns very closely to both instructional and participative leadership as the communication of teachers in school often revolves around the students' progress and their classroom interactions.

Leadership is not confined to certain roles in the organization, but flows through various networks of roles, all intertwined in the organization. When teachers form groups to engage themselves in the all-round growth and development of students, then many issues get resolved with informal discussions. With the responsibility of pedagogical leadership, teachers have a great social influence on how students look at the process of teaching and how they learn. Since their leadership is not for one but for all, it takes into account an egalitarian view of leadership.

Leadership by teachers gets demonstrated in many informal ways such as coaching peers to resolve instructional problems, encouraging parent participation, working with colleagues in teams and modelling reflective practices. They have myriad opportunities to practise leadership every day in the school. I know of a school where some of the mentor teachers are so effective that the other teachers refer the parents of students in their own class to them to amicably solve their students' issues. One such student who faced problems was a Grade 6 boy who often got into serious brawls in that school. His parents refused to acknowledge that the child suffered from ADHD (Attention Deficit Hyperactive Disorder) and needed regular psychological intervention such as undergoing a Behaviour Modification Programme.

Even after the child's numerous visits to the school counsellor and meeting of his parents with the principal, nothing much changed in the student's violent behaviour. However, recently, the child hit a class fellow with such ferociousness that shockingly blood flowed from the victim's wound, his face badly bruised. After immediate medical attention was given to him, parents were called to the school to discuss the issue. It was rather disconcerting that the parents of the precocious child continued to defend their child under all kinds of justification, ranging from teachers' inefficiency, school policies, his class fellows' behaviour and the provocative comment of the child who was hit. However, school policies prevailed and the child was appropriately censured.

Teachers dealing with such parents often feel helpless since they do not respect the school ethos and systems. In this case, the school finally placed the child under the tutelage of a teacher who is especially known for her expertise in dealing with such children and guiding the parents very firmly. She has been such a success with the child that many teachers approach her now to deal with such conflicts in their classes. The teacher clearly has leadership qualities due to which parents listen to her, appreciate her no-nonsense viewpoint and look at her with greater respect even when she is drawing their attention to their parenting qualities or rather a lack of them.

It is commonplace to see how some teachers during a Parent Teacher Meeting (PTM) are much more sought after than others since they have demonstrated the ability to lead and mentor students. In school programmes ranging from annual functions to investiture ceremonies as well as school assemblies, it is always very obvious who the teacher leaders are in the school since they come forward on their own to share responsibilities and see that they are carried out. Similarly, those teachers, who lead programmes of professional development in schools, gradually assume teacher leadership qualities since they work closely with many teachers and learn from their experiences of collaboration. Modelling and encouraging professional growth of their peers by conducting workshops, they naturally assume the role of teacher leaders.

Teachers who lead the examination department also begin to lead effectively and address many a problem faced by students and teachers. Teacher leaders lead regardless of their position or title. They continuously strive for authenticity in their teaching, learning and assessment practices. They do not even hesitate to confront and surmount barriers in the school's culture and structures, translating ideas into sustainable solutions with confidence.

A qualitative research project was conducted in six elementary schools of Florida, with in-depth interviews with teachers. The detailed interviews spanning three months asked questions about the roles these teachers play, how much decision-making they do, how they define teacher expertise, what the power relations in their schools are and their insights about what they value in a teacher. Teacher leaders were found to have different means of agency through which they accomplished change in the school. These included advocacy, fairness, enabling others, professionalism, relationships and innovation. These teachers worked within and across the school boundaries and structures to establish social linkages and networks among their peers and the larger community. Their stories illustrate that those teachers who exert the most agency in this study are treated with greater trust and respect by their peers. They have the most empowering principals in the schools. That enables them to have more autonomy, which brings them opportunities to be more creative.

Power equations can transform school cultures. Teachers cannot feel empowered unless they accept the power given to them. Conversely, principals must know how to create conditions that foster empowerment with accountability. To achieve this, principals have to release their control over teachers by reducing surveillance and micromanagement of day-to-day activities.

In many other studies, the characteristic that stands out for inculcating teacher leadership is collaboration, which has the largest impact. For example, all the curriculum development and management work is led by teacher leaders in each school. Within a department, there are different degrees of leadership that the teachers teaching a particular subject possess. Most often, teachers who are participative in administrative tasks and adept at monitoring improvement efforts, get entrusted with curriculum management. A formal position or the absence of it, does not affect real teacher leadership. Over a period of time when other teachers demonstrate high levels of instructional expertise, reflection and a sense of empowerment, their peers allow them to lead. They are learners themselves and exert a lot of natural influence on their peers. Besides their excellent teaching skills and also being at a career stage that enables them to give others all their time and effort, these teachers build ties of collegiality with their peers. That is why many senior teachers in schools assume the role of teacher leaders. However, seniority and age by themselves are not the criteria for developing teachers as leaders. Many mid-career teachers also take up leading roles by their high energy levels and great zeal displayed in carrying out school responsibilities. They have a clearly developed personal philosophy of education which they bring to their work practices and informal discussions.

Sensitivity and receptivity to the thoughts and feelings of others help them to build trust and a meaningful rapport with colleagues for building solid relationships. When they are supportive of their colleagues and promote their growth, they find acceptance in these groups of teachers. Among the most important traits of teacher leadership are effective communication and empathetic listening skills.

School culture has a dominant influence on the success initiatives of a school. Frequent and ongoing opportunities have to be provided to shape the role of teacher leaders. When the principal is not visible or present to give feedback, it would be rare to find teachers growing as leaders. Norms of teamwork and a culture of communication have the deepest influence on building teacher leaders—collegiality and openness build a culture of learning, inquiry and reflective practice. On the other hand, norms of isolation and individualism create reluctant leaders. A highly impeding factor in building teacher leadership is the 'crab bucket culture' in which teachers drag each other down instead of supporting and inspiring one another.

As a young and zealous head of the department of geography in a leading school of Delhi, I managed to excite and enthuse students about learning the subject. Instead of following textbooks strictly, I showed them video clips as well as movies that had real geographical features from around the world and took them on various field trips where they could learn geographical concepts in real settings with hands-on experience. While teaching economic and political geography, I took some initiatives, such as discussing the current affairs of the country and the world with students, encouraging them to express their views.

I found my reputation soaring high among the other departments as much appreciation came my way through students and the school principal. However, instead of letting me grow further, many senior teachers took to the 'crab bucket culture' where obstacles were thrown my way while I was trying to bring in a fresh perspective to the subject. The senior teachers did not take well to the accolades coming in within a few months for my new ways of teaching. I was disheartened. Here was I as an upcoming teacher leader, respected by students and their parents as well as many colleagues, but the prevailing deep culture of dissuading new teachers from growing curtailed my wings of flight.

In some schools, the view is fostered that teachers who take on leadership roles are stepping out of line. Conflicts and power struggles are the salient features of the 'crab bucket culture'. Clearly, teacher leadership cannot develop in schools where well-entrenched cartels of senior teachers feel threatened by new and promising teachers. Hierarchical, instead of horizontal, relationships with peers stifle teacher leadership. The traditional top-down structure of leadership also does not foster the growth and development of teacher leaders. As a result, many schools suffer from a lack of home-grown talent for second-rung positions or the top position since they have never allowed any promotion of future leadership.

Lack of incentives or rewards for engaging in leadership activities also does not help the cause of teacher leadership. The senior management needs to invest in many possible ways to encourage teachers to lead. It is all very well to have intrinsic motivation but what is also required is the public recognition of talent and effort. Schools may vary in their approach to incentivize teachers who take greater responsibility not only by giving them monetary benefits but also through many other ways, such as sending them for international conferences which help them gain a wider perspective. Some other schools give them opportunities to study further and train themselves through funded programmes. Yet others put them on the succession ladder to gain senior leadership positions.

Schools where principals and the senior management develop a culture of appreciation and motivation will always have a great many teachers assuming the roles of teacher leaders. It is clear that wherever teacher leadership flourishes, principals have actively supported or at least encouraged it. Empowering principals fosters empowerment of teachers and engender commitment, trust and respect in the school. Thus, the principal's role is to be redefined from instructional leadership to a developer of the community of leaders.

Developing teacher leadership is the first step in developing professional learning communities—it is inextricably connected to teacher learning and is not for a few but for all. Teachers who become leaders, experience personal and professional satisfaction, a reduction in isolation, a sense of instrumentality and new learnings, all of which spill over into their teaching. We cannot achieve quality learning for all students until quality development is attained and sustained for all teachers.

# 11

# Leading with Equity and Participation

Ideas about democratic leadership developed in the late 1930s, with the experiment undertaken by psychologists Kurt Lewin and Ronald Lippitt in the USA. In the experiment, three groups of school children operated under three differential leadership styles: authoritarian, democratic and laissez-faire. The authoritarian leader offered clear expectations about what would be done, when and how, with minimum inputs from other group members. The democratic leader offered guidance to group members by participating and encouraging member involvement in the decision-making process, while the laissez-faire leader offered little or no guidance to group members, leaving all decision-making to group members. Common activity projects were given to each member of each group so that they could be observed. Democratic leadership group members were found to be more engaged and motivated, working creatively and collaboratively and freely expressing their ideas and actions strengthened collegiality. The members of the authoritarian group were found to be less creative, more dissatisfied and uninvolved and similarly, the members in the laissez-faire group were the least productive with the lowest achievement and satisfaction.

Of central importance within schools striving for continuous improvement is a shared set of values. When the personal vision and belief system of the principal gets communicated by direction, words and deeds through a variety of symbolic gestures and action, democratic leadership takes root. Leaders who 'walk the talk' through the consistency and integrity of their actions in order to model the behaviour are able to achieve goals with respect and trust for all the staff and the students. Such leaders believe that people are their greatest assets and maintain staff morale and motivation at all times, creating a 'can do' culture. Their openness, fairness and honesty sparkle through each interaction of theirs. Ultimately, the most important task of a leader is to give confidence and instil the capability to take on new responsibilities. It is devolved leadership which does not believe in power and control but empowering and encouraging the others to act in the best interest of the school (Fig. 11).

In schools where democratic approaches are embraced, all school members engage to work as a team in the decision-making, implementation and monitoring processes. Such leadership opens up the boundaries of leadership beyond those in formal leadership positions. It utilizes the expertise and initiative of all members in a way that benefits the whole school, going beyond what the school leaders can achieve alone.

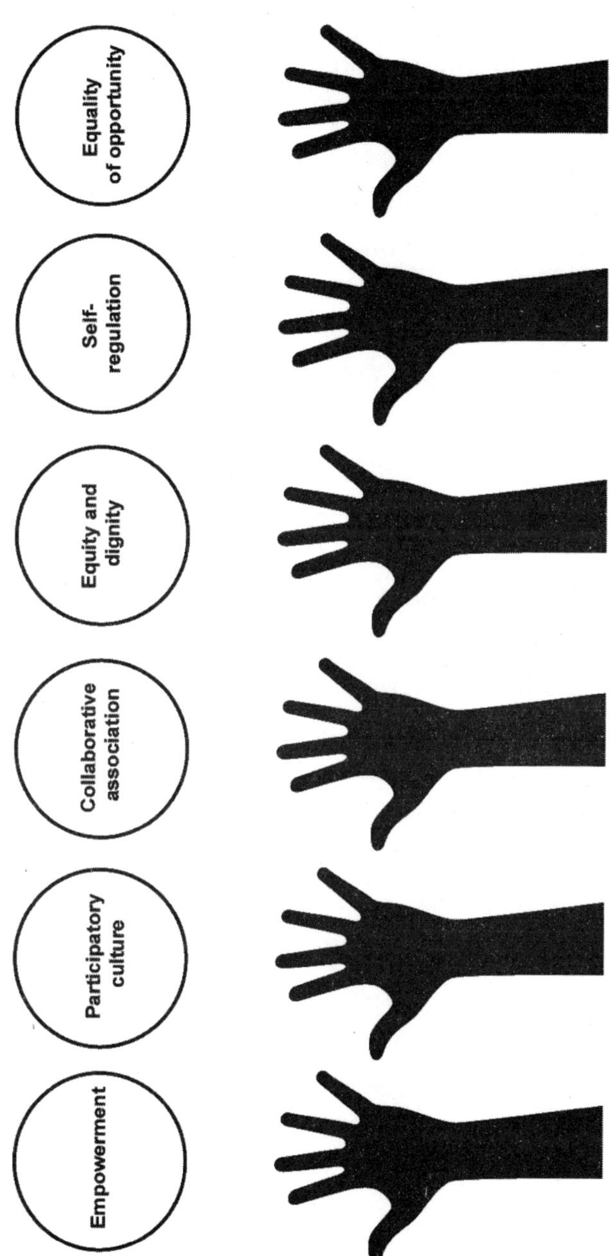


Fig. 11: Democratic Leadership

Respectful relationships, collaborative association, active cooperation and meaningful participation are some of the salient features of democratic leadership. Indeed, democratic leadership implies that it is the responsibility of school principals to build educational organizations around central democratic values such as supporting the equity, dignity, rights and welfare of all individuals in the school. It is a way of life in which community norms and values are continually held open to informed critique, diversity is recognized, and change is expected. The open flow of ideas, regardless of their popularity, enables people to be as fully informed as possible. Creating a democratic community in schools is a systemic challenge, involving structures, processes and curriculum. Empowerment can be achieved by creating a stimulating environment where students also develop as responsible citizens.

A correlational study was conducted in Turkish high schools which included a sample of 462 teachers from 22 schools, exploring the democratic and distributed leadership perceptions of their leadership. Descriptive statistics and exploratory factor analysis were used to determine the extent of democratic and distributed leadership in schools. The findings of this study indicate that there is a strong relationship between democratic leadership and coherent team characteristics, concluding that when democratic leadership is present, teams are more coherent and cohesive. Democracy adds to the emergent character of distributed leadership functions such as support and supervision. Democratic leadership is the first step towards building a future of distributed leadership in schools.

In many countries, the efforts made to improve schools have illustrated that neither top-down measures alone nor the exclusive use of bottom-up approach have the desired impact. Instead, a combination and systematic synchronization of both has proved most effective. To make improvement a continuous process, innovations need to be institutionalized after their initiation, so that they become a permanent part of the school culture. Hence, the goal is to develop problem-solving, creative and self-renewing schools that are the real learning organizations. The essential change agents in this process are teachers and school leaders. Democracy and cooperation represent a rationale for actions concerning the intrinsic willingness and motivation of staff and pupils. This implies the active, co-determining and collaborative participation of all, so that leaders are able to empower and enable staff and students to assume the responsibility for teaching and learning.

During the last three years, the school, which I was heading, was used to a very centralized system of working where everything had to be 'told' to get done. Teachers had no clue that they could take up any initiative for students and the overall improvement of the school. It was strange for me to see a great many parents waiting to meet with the principal in the beginning, for reasons varying from student absence, academic status, examination issue, and so on. The first thing that I initiated in the school was to designate people for various responsibilities wherein they could take a decision to the best of their ability and rope me in only when absolutely necessary. Why, for instance, the examination in charge could not take a decision on how to deal with a student for missing an exam and the action to be followed, was beyond my comprehension. Similarly, various departmental heads and coordinators were there in the school but they all worked without any onus of decision-making. They even said that they were afraid of taking decisions on their own from the fear of any untoward repercussion. That defeated the entire purpose of decentralization. Clearly, there was a need for building more trust in the school between the principal and teachers for everyone to believe that they would be supported for their decisions.

I was pleasantly surprised once when a parent came to meet with me even after the issue had already been resolved by the coordinator. I asked him if there was anything more that I could do for him. He just wanted to be sure that the decision had credibility with the stamp of the principal's assent. It took some time for the parent body in general to believe that once any matter pertaining to their child, big or small, had been addressed by the person concerned, the principal stood by it. Often, in staff meetings I reiterated to teachers that even when some minor errors are made, we can all collectively learn from them but that shouldn't take away their decision-making. In due course, it became a common practice in the school for teachers to take responsibility with accountability. Since they had never before experienced this democracy in the school, they took time to gain confidence. However, it started showing results in the school efficiency without any undue delay caused by the authority vested in only one person.

A democratic leader's goal is to develop pupils' independent thinking, to make them self-responsible and socially responsible future citizens. Over a period of time, these students start feeling accountable about working towards attaining the aims of the school. For instance, there are leaders who create a vision for environment sustainability in schools. Walking the talk themselves, they are able to inculcate these values among staff and students. They are able to inspire school members to think of the larger community around them and share the responsibility of the world's well-being.

In a setting of democratic leadership, democracy is lived through participation in the everyday practice of school life. The delicate and difficult task of developing character and good judgement in the young needs every stimulus and inspiration possible. When teachers and students find the prevalence of democratic habits and thought as the fibre of the organization, they build more cohesive social relationships. Encouraging the pupil's voice to become an important ingredient in the functioning of the school goes a long way in democratizing the school. When students know they can write to the principal, meet with her for any discussion and walk into her office if something is urgent, they see those values being lived. I asked them in the assemblies if they really needed a suggestion box on every floor to put in their complaints anonymously. Could they not instead articulate them to their teachers or the principal without any feeling of threat? They agreed, albeit with trepidation initially, because every new change takes time to gain roots. They had to be told that democracy belongs to those who exercise it. It is always a process in the making, founded in possibilities which we only need to explore. When students set up the class rules themselves and submit them to the teacher, the class gets more conducive for learning. When they check each other for using plastic in their daily lives, they live the ethos of sustainability. All that is required is teachers' support and belief in them to get these values internalized. I am convinced that pupils' voice is the road to change education.

Today, EWS students study along with other comparatively better-off students. How the school leadership deals with them through their everyday decisions and routines goes a long way in establishing democratic norms in the school. When students experience equality of opportunities in every walk of school life, they imbibe these values for a long time to come till these values become an integral part of their character. Teachers who are fair and transparent in dealing with the inequality of students' background further strengthen the culture of equity and social justice in the school.

It cannot be overemphasized that school leaders' own value system and beliefs in social equity affect the climate of the school. When the welfare of all and the common good become the values of school, they reflect in students' achievement and teachers' attitudes towards their pupils. Such schools continue to strive for equalizing educational attainment for the vulnerable section of students with empathy and responsiveness. Irrespective of the family's economic and social background, each student in such schools feels more integrated into the institutional fabric. They are more committed to the vision of the school and try to accomplish the shared goals.

On the other hand, where social cohesion is weak and discrimination is visible, EWS students face an identity crisis.

They remain secluded and develop a disordered perspective about themselves. Since the values of democracy get conveyed to teachers and through them to students by the leadership in the school, democratic leadership reduces the stratification in schooling by making them more inclusive. To develop egalitarian values across the members of the institution, the onus lies on the school leadership. When students are not discriminated against on the basis of their ability to pay, their educational attainment rises.

As the head of a continuous professional development programme for four schools of a leading chain of schools in India, I had the first-hand experience of working in a very democratic setup. The chairman of the school not only believed in egalitarianism but practised it for all to see and follow. He did not discriminate against any staff member on the parochial lines of economic background, status, caste, creed or religion, a practice that was particularly important because the schools worked in highly divided societies across the country. Every person was recognized for the contribution made towards the organization, whether he was a janitor or coordinator of the school, principal or a newly recruited teacher. In the annual luncheon hosted by him for the entire school, one could see all the organizational members interacting and mingling with each other, leading to a perfectly cohesive and synchronized team. Although the schools worked in a highly diverse society, over a period of time they became the beacons of equity, fairness and social justice in each city they were situated in. It is not surprising, therefore, that every single member of the schools wanted to contribute to the best of their abilities since they identified well with the vision of the chairman.

Today, these schools, even though spread over different geographies of the country, continue to rank among the finest in the country. Clearly, it was a perfect example of enlightened leadership oriented towards the constitutional aspects of the country. Students didn't have to be given special lessons on the values of democracy since they observed and lived them through their daily interactions. The supportive culture of the schools across economic and social classes turned them into trusting organizations, living examples of the principle of collegiality with shared obligations pertaining to organizational goals. All stakeholders were integrated into a single whole, focused on achieving excellence for the schools. In my opinion, this was an empowering way of creating an organization geared towards meaningful learning.

Democratic leadership, therefore, democratizes decision-making processes, conflict management, problem-solving, interpretations of regulations as well as everyday routines of the school. Built on the premise of participation, relationship orientation and consideration for subordinates, it helps in creating autonomy for all stakeholders, sharing power and information with due processes in the organizational structure. Schools that are continuously striving for significant gains in student learning require the active engagement of all stakeholders. Clearly, school leadership extends beyond the person of the principal to all levels.

# 12

# Inspiring Loyalty and Motivating Change Through Charisma

Also referred to as 'heroic leadership', charismatic leadership is the method of encouraging particular behaviours in followers by way of eloquent communication, persuasion and force of personality. Max Weber, the father of sociology, first coined the term 'Charisma', originally taken from Greek *Kharisma*, which means a divine gift. Body language communicates a person's emotions and motivations, interest and disengagement. When a person is most charismatic and convincing, he or she is perfectly aligned with what is being expressed verbally. Charismatic leaders use a wide range of their expressions such as genuine smiles, positive eye contact and a variety of gestures to convey non-verbal warmth and openness. We just know charisma when we see it. Charismatic leaders motivate an organization's members to get things done by conjuring up eagerness in others to achieve a stated goal. They appeal to the emotions of people in a profound way to articulate their vision. They have a distinct ability to decipher any inefficiency in the organization, often resulting from their critical thinking, compilation of facts and finding ways to solve a variety of problems.

Charisma is essentially an interface between the characteristics of a charismatic leader and the followers who identify themselves with their leader. Charismatic leaders are most often experienced, drawing from their wisdom and knowledge accumulated over the years. Confident in their abilities, they inspire great loyalty from their followers as they are able to transform the needs, values, preferences and aspirations of their followers from self-interest to collective interest. The followers are willing even to make personal sacrifices for such leaders, which means that commitment is generally high in such organizations.

The first theoretical explanation of the impact of charismatic leadership on followers goes back much further in time, to the writings of Greek philosopher Aristotle in the 4th century. Aristotle laid the foundation of the field of rhetoric, which is a key foundation of charismatic leadership. He argues in *Rhetoric* that leaders rouse followers' emotions (the 'Pathos'), providing a moral perspective through personal character (the 'Ethos'), and using reasoned argument (the 'Logos'). However, Max Weber, who, as mentioned earlier, is credited with coining the term 'Charisma' in 1947 while describing the charismatic leader as one who could bring about social change. He is of the opinion that the specific gifts of a charismatic leader are not accessible to everyone. These leaders are attributed with superhuman or at least specifically exceptional qualities.

The followers willingly place their destiny in their leader's hands and support his mission with great enthusiasm. It is interesting to see the hint of a salvationary quest of followers in the context of a charismatic leader. Trust gets solidified as psychological exchanges occur between the charismatic leader and the followers. They are so invested in such a leader that their quest borders on sheer reverence. They come forward with inspirational commitment for the causes espoused by the charismatic leader.

Such leaders draw upon the moral realm of leadership by inspiring followers with their extraordinary vision for change. An Australian case study illustrates the influence of charismatic leadership in a school which had students with multiple disabilities from 1986 to 2009. The principal of this specialist school achieved extraordinary feats for the school and students. When she retired in 2009, she had transformed the school from a neighbourhood establishment in a converted home with just 20 students to a magnificent facility with an innovative curriculum, a worldwide reputation and 150 students. She challenged prejudice in the community towards students with disabilities. Her passion to create a world-class special school meant that she often fought the education department bureaucracy to gain autonomy to make decisions and obtain resources beyond what would normally be available. The most notable achievement included transformation of the school site with a state-of-the-art building, equipment, resources and facilities.

She established Australia's first fully integrated service model to support disabled students and their families. Most importantly, with her magnetism, she was successful in changing the school culture from one of 'caring' and 'therapy' to that of 'education and learning'. Indeed a 'visionary doer', she demonstrated a range of interpersonal skills such as flexibility, teamwork, motivation, patience and active listening to the various stakeholders to build relationships within the school and with the wider community. She could negotiate the allocation of resources to her dream school from the education department with the help of conflict management strategies. More importantly, her self-confidence opened doors to possibilities.

Compassion, fortitude, honesty and integrity are qualities that charismatic leaders exhibit. Without substance, charisma can exist but only for a short period of time. These leaders not only talk the talk but also walk the walk. Comfortable in their own skin and confident as they are, they are people who believe a glass is half full. Since they are able to emotionally arouse the values of followers, intrinsic motivation is often

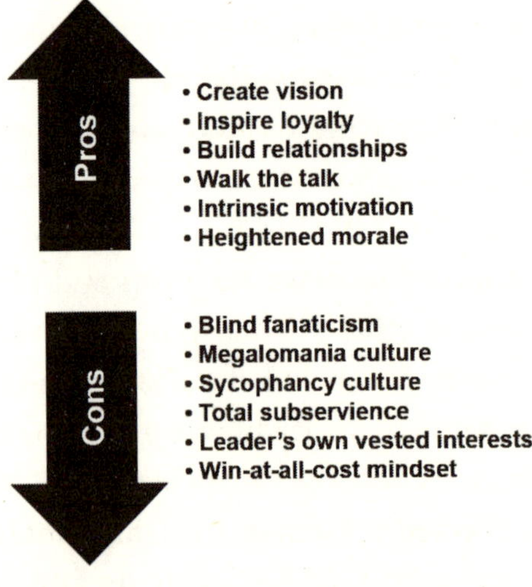


**Fig. 12: Charismatic Leadership**

the result among followers, who rise above their own self-interest for the larger good (Fig. 12). As these leaders understand themselves well, they are authentic and do not try to be someone else. Conscious of their image, they self-monitor themselves to sustain their powerful personality. Besides, well aware of the qualities that get them attention, they continue to hone them.

The famous challenge of American President John F. Kennedy, 'Ask not what your country can do for you—ask what you can do for your country' envisions charismatic leadership well. Such leaders increase effort-accomplishment expectancies by gradually enhancing the follower's self-esteem and self-worth. A better sense of self-worth adds to the feeling of self-efficacy. A stronger group identity also emerges among team members. Subtle and spontaneous learning occurs when relevant messages are inferred by followers from observation of their leaders' behaviour, lifestyle, emotional reactions—all conveyed by liberal use of the tools of symbolism, mysticism, imagery and fantasy. This messaging is strong and gives people a hope for the future and a belief that it is legitimate to develop. The leader then becomes an ideal, a point of reference in followers' conversation, turning into a beacon who can resolve shortcomings and mobilize the process of change.

These leaders are celebrated as heroes and are believed to be able to turn around any organization. They are viewed as a magic elixir to cure organizational woes and change the course of events. They instil faith in a better future for followers, exhorting them to transcend limits beyond their existence and vision. In fact, they de-emphasize extrinsic rewards, encouraging followers to feel internally motivated to reach the goal articulated by such leaders. Intellectual stimulation is a very strong characteristic of charismatic leaders, resulting in the percolation of heightened motivation, positive affects towards the leader, support for leader policies and self-assurance in the organization. Relational trust runs high and the connect between the leader and followers gets strengthened. A higher work-engagement results in overall organizational improvement.

While the virtues of charismatic leaders are extolled in popular leadership and management literature, there is also a potential dark side of these leaders which is often ignored. The label 'charismatic' has also been applied to a very diverse set of leaders from Jesus Christ, Mahatma Gandhi, Dr Martin Luther King Jr, Lee Iacocca to even Adolf Hitler and Benito Mussolini. This means that the risks involved in charismatic leadership are as large as the promises.

Charisma can lead to blind fanaticism in the service of megalomaniacs who have dangerous ends in mind. Kim Jong-un, the supreme leader of North Korea, succeeded his megalomaniac father Kim Jong-il. He has continued to follow the same cult of personality as his father and grandfather, treating the entire country as his personal fiefdom. He has ordered the purge of several North Korean officials and expanded the nuclear programme to threaten the world peace by launching missiles and rockets. The country remains isolated from the world, behind a strong iron curtain. Its citizens, starved and malnourished, live in servitude, but the country continues to expand its military prowess to choreograph its misplaced might to the world.

Kim Jong-un is responsible for several human rights violation, where his country's top officials either live in perpetual fear of being executed or defect from the country for political asylum. His luxurious lifestyle is completely in stark contrast to the state of deprivation in which the citizens live. The State TV's only mandate is to promote the cult of the 'Dear Leader' with overexcited reading of news, showing genuflecting people, completely in awe of the leader, everything obviously stage-crafted as well as state-crafted. The totalitarian state has most unusual laws, which when flouted lead to the person's execution. This is the dark side of a charismatic leader.

We then have to be careful about the unethical side of charismatic leadership so that informed decisions are made by followers, as self-serving charismatic leaders can do more harm than good to an organization. They can manipulate people for furthering their personal agenda and undue promotions. They censure critical views in the organization, expecting total agreement for every policy, keeping communication on a one-way path to avoid debates. Having an inflated sense of self-importance, they thrive on attention and admiration from others and shun contrary views. Sycophancy is the result of such leadership in the organization since uncritical followers gravitate towards them, expecting benefits. Over a period of time, these followers lose their self-confidence, hesitant to question the leader's thinking and decisions. This magnifies their complete dependence on the leader, making them decidedly obedient, dependent and compliant, undermining their motivation and ability to challenge the existing views. Slowly, such leadership can degenerate into a dominant and authoritarian style where power is used for personal ends.

As the above-mentioned example of North Korea suggests, a country led by a megalomaniac will lead to unprecedented suffering for its people. Would that not be true also for a school where a megalomaniac leader sees nothing beyond his/her own power, forgetting what he/she ought to have done for the students, teachers and the community?

Ethical charismatic leaders create and express the vision that contributes to the shared goals of their followers. They transfer their dreams only to get people to accept the concept to attain a common good, not for vested interests. They continuously seek feedback and viewpoints, developing a two-way interaction process. Open communication is the key since they learn from criticism. They ask their followers to question the 'tried and tested' ways of solving problems. It is not surprising, therefore, that such leaders recognize the potential in their team members and give them opportunities to develop it, trusting their abilities and competencies. They are not swayed by popular opinion unless it is in line with their principles, the level of ethics slowly rising in the organization since they are seen to be transparent and fair, not getting carried away by select people. Their internal consistency sets standards which everyone buys into as they are predictable. They do not falter in their duties irrespective of popular opinion.

Adherence to ethical principles is the key in such organizations. They are not 'win-at-all-costs' people, moving roughshod over everyone without a thought. They know that the best form of leadership builds followers into leaders who eventually take responsibility for their own ethical behaviour, development and performance. They have a positive relationship with work engagement in the organization, leading to better organizational behaviour.

However, charismatic leadership often becomes incompatible with the onset of increasingly competitive and knowledge-intensive economy. Australian management consultant and author Peter Drucker, whose writings contributed to the philosophical and practical foundations of modern business corporations, had famously said that charisma becomes the undoing of leaders and makes them inflexible, convinced of their own infallibility. The new paradigm distributes leadership among stakeholders committed to democratic practices who also display their agency for achieving effective and socially just change in the organization. Most schools prefer a more nuanced version of leadership which is collective and collegial. Having said that, charismatic leadership remains alive and well today despite the recognized expansion and transition to post-heroic leadership.

# 13

# Impelling Movement Towards Betterment of the School

A leader whose aim is change for the better can bring about all-pervading reforms into a school, rather than just maintaining the status quo. Motion leadership is the ability to move individuals, institutions and the whole system forward. The motion leader is driven with a sense of movement in positive and desired directions and can achieve transformation. Educational consultant and author Michael Fullan, who propounded the theoretical framework for motion leadership, identified six strategies that must be implemented in a school to effectively bring about a sense of perpetual moving forward. These include leading the movement in the right direction, collaboration, and forging relationships even if there is resistance. Motion leaders love their employees and focus on relationships. They believe in the relationships built on trust, convinced that everything else will follow once the relationships among team members are stronger. Every association in the school, whether it is between the principal and teachers, school and parents, teacher and students, thrives with this relational trust. When every stakeholder knows that he is loved, valued and appreciated, he will go the extra mile to participate in the change process. If the leader fails to build relationships on mutual respect and trust, students and teachers are less likely to follow the vision of the organization, since the sense of a whole community is only built with these close-knit associations.

Relationship building is not easy. It takes time and effort on the part of each individual concerned. When the principal models building of relationships in the school, it percolates down to the last person. Trust supports effective communication, an ability to collaborate across departments and hierarchies, the willingness to seek fair solutions to difficult situations and the overall ability of all stakeholders to have confidence in the leader's vision (Fig. 13). How does trust grow? When everyone in the organization perceives others as credible—that what they say is true, their actions are consistent with their words and that they will be ethical in their practices—trust evolves. Trust also depends on how much employees experience respect, through support provided for professional development.

When teachers see they are being included in the decision-making process, they start trusting the leader and each other. I would like to give an example from my school here. Besides leading the school as the principal, I also direct the department of teachers' training for 10 schools under the educational trust which runs these schools. Teachers had been attending various training programmes for years,

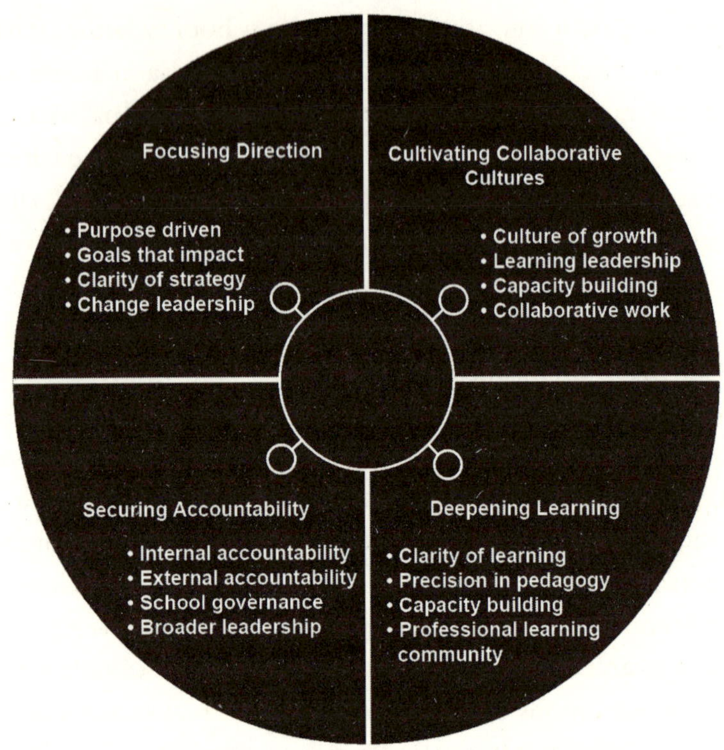


**Fig. 13: Motion Leadership**

as I came to know at the time of joining. However, they had never thought that some of them could also develop as master trainers for their own schools and beyond. When I constituted a group of passionate and highly motivated teachers to sign in for a master trainers programme, only a few names came forth. Not to be deterred by the number, the programme started with regular meetings and training modules for a year. These apprentice master trainers used to then conduct programmes in their own schools, which became so popular that within a year, more teachers expressed their interest in training. It was so heartening to see that the momentum that started for being coached as master trainers infused new enthusiasm in teachers with a feeling of self-efficacy. It can be said with conviction after three years of starting this programme that teachers not only bought into the idea of being pedagogical trainers themselves but moved many others to enrol in the programme.

Trust also grows through the sense that regardless of the position or personal characteristics of a teacher, everyone will be treated fairly and equitably for opportunities. A feeling of pride in the organization combined with a sense of camaraderie, of being a part of a large family or team, further solidifies trust. By observing workplace interactions between teachers and the principal, teachers and students, the school and parents, we are able to see how much trust is present. Therefore, to build relationships in the school, both emotional and rational actions are required. The emotions associated with it include affection, gratitude, security, confidence, acceptance, admiration, respect, appreciation, contentment and satisfaction. The rationale of this is grounded in the assessment of a person's dependability, which plays a significant role in building trust. Organizations based on high trust correlate positively with high degrees of personnel involvement, commitment and organizational success. It gives a sense of heightened loyalty, powerful energy, strong innovation, robust engagement, increased adaptability and high retention. Trusting leaders say 'we' and they think 'team'. They accept responsibility, never sidestepping it.

The school that I was heading in Punjab was in every possible way a green school. Its everyday practices were sustainable, the building was weather-ambient, the attitudes of students and teachers were eco-friendly. Once I asked the eco-club teachers if their work could be geared to winning a national award for the school. They came up with a project idea which initially looked daunting to everyone. However, one of the teachers was so passionate about the project that she asked me if I could support her, promising that once I gave her that assurance, she would move mountains! She might have said this metaphorically but with her team of committed students and many peers, she indeed moved mountains, almost literally.

Together we found a dried-up pond in a village nearby—it once used to be full of water but unscientific practices of farming and acute apathy of people had turned it into a small slush pit from what it originally used to be. We had numerous meetings with the villagers, the panchayat head and other office-bearers, where the students put forth their idea to them. Albeit sceptically, they agreed and gave us their assent. Students and teachers began with clearing out plastic and other wastes that had accumulated in the pond over the years and slowly began the process of revival. A large area was dug up manually as well as mechanically, trees planted around it, the women of the village also joining in along with their children.

It took six months of continuous work after school hours for us to get that dead pond come to life again with flowing water from the monsoons. We aptly called it the Blue Pond and then with a lot of fanfare, it was inaugurated by the villagers themselves. The teacher who led the project had a never-say-die attitude with her penchant for moving people and, of course, moving mountains. Tons of earth excavated every day was sent to the surrounding villages to be used as a new layer of soil. From these villages, more people came in and joined the mission. Incredibly, she got a team of dedicated students and teachers in this dream project and what a perfect culmination it had—the Centre for Science and Environment gave the school a National Award in the Bhagidari (partnership) category of environmental projects, thus recognizing the achievement. This shows that there are indeed teachers who can be motion leaders themselves.

Thus, motion leaders connect peers with purpose. Teachers should see their connections with each other for which motion leaders create opportunities. Strong professional bonds form among teachers when they collaborate on projects and activities, instead of working in silos. Such leaders help in building professional learning communities, whose members learn from each other. In such environments, there are frequent conversations among teachers about pedagogy with consistent and well-defined expectations for students, heightened by their visits to each other's classrooms to observe and critique instruction. If properly implemented, professional learning communities have the wherewithal to transform the entire school.

Motion leaders also provide time for collaborative activities, which may include developing and aligning the curriculum, sharing instructional practices, making assessments, analysing data and participating in peer observation. When principals take active part in teachers' professional development, they help in connecting teachers with each other for a common purpose. Shared leadership practices further enhance collaboration. Such opportunities help teachers to engage students in rigorous learning which requires critical thinking skills. Motion leaders create a climate of cooperation that flourishes with support and lends energy to the success of the school community.

Motion leadership fosters capacity building of knowledge, skills and dispositions of people, both individually and collectively. When principals encourage development of leadership across the organization, integrated teams start developing, which routinely share their learning with others. More teachers participating in and sharing responsibility for various categories of school operations result in utility of purpose and strategic focus in school functioning. Schools thrive when principals play a major role in developing the capacity of all stakeholders.

Owing to the lopsided policies of the Delhi government, the last school where I worked had not been able to hike its tuition fee annually for the last five years due to which new recruitment of teachers and other personnel had got stalled. When the only front office person went on maternity leave, the school had no one to manage visitors, telephonic queries and other administrative matters. One of the teachers, who is a special educator, volunteered to carry out those responsibilities till the person returned on duty which could have taken any amount of time, beyond her six months leave. Without knowing what she had to do and what she was in for, she stood up for the school vision and contributed towards its functioning, even if that meant relearning and reskilling. In the process, she learnt writing business letters, sending official emails, dealing with irate parents, numerous visitors and handling phone calls, but every evening when she left for home, she still smiled. Besides, she never missed any online class of hers with the special children. Did she ever think of the difference in the position of a special trainer educator and that of an office assistant? Did her endeavour result from the training with special children which needs patience and empathy or was it her own attitude towards work? Whatever it was, clearly, schools that are moving ahead, never stop for any reason. They continue with their forward movement.

Through a leadership team approach, school leaders can build numerous other leaders by empowering them to participate in school growth, inspiring them to become competent in their practice, encouraging their collaboration and creating partnerships both within and beyond the school walls for everyone's benefit. Coaching and mentoring, the two personal development methods employed by leaders, help in capacity building. They nurture a person's own ability to improve behaviour and performance. There are subtle but significant differences in their aim, emphasis and style. Coaching is more task-oriented, skill-focused and time-bound while mentoring is about open-ended personal development.

Principals can coach their teachers with the help of a short-term intervention aimed at performance improvement or developing a particular competence. They can go beyond coaching through mentoring by supporting people to manage their own learning in order to maximize their potential to become the person they want to be. Transformational attributes of leadership are necessary for both coaching and mentoring. For effective mentoring, transformational leaders graduate from one level of leadership to another, until they reach the pinnacle of achievement.

Continuous learning is the work that school leaders and teachers must persevere with. Motivation to learn at every possible opportunity is the role that action leaders can model for all the stakeholders, making the relentless pursuit of implementing the vision a priority. In efficient schools, although systems are in place, goals are set and the vision is clear to everyone, the effort towards excellence is never over. To maintain the same level of collaboration among professional learning communities of the school, monitoring students' learning, guiding the instruction and making adjustments based on the data collected, leadership in motion is required. To lead schools to greatness, the commitment required is at every level in the school—of course, starting from the top. Motion leaders are driven to do whatever it takes to make the school a model one. High-yielding learning practices are constantly found out, discussed, practised and implemented in the school. The relentless consistency of such a leadership has the most visible impact on school success.

—∞—

The next step towards excellence is to follow the rules of transparency. There must be a clear and continuous display of results and the instructional practices that produce results. Everyone must have access to data which should be used as a tool for improvement. School leaders must confront the honest truth about what the data says. Ignoring the data and making decisions without it is like the emperor's new clothes which are said to be grand but are not present in reality.

Leaders, who are data-literate and proficient in handling it, become transparent effortlessly. Organizations run the risk of getting obsolete without transparency. Increased transparency brings increased awareness, coherence and comprehensibility to information exchanged among all stakeholders of the school. In order to gain trust, instead of just trying to convince people about a point of view, one has to maintain transparency in planning and actions to have greater influence over stakeholders. What is even more important is the fact that leaders must not simply 'pass along' information but also have knowledgeable opinion and expertise about the issues being discussed. Also, there must be a willingness to be vulnerable or exposed and to take risks in allowing others to see the planning process where the entire group has a chance to voice opinions and concerns. No one should be beyond scrutiny. Leaders have to be forthcoming about the motives for the decisions made, which gives them a moral imperative to lead.

A report of the Organization for Economic Co-operation and Development (OECD), 'Education Policy Outlook: Finland', in 2013, on the key Finnish context and features that make for successful schooling outcomes throws some interesting findings on school culture. In Finland, a strong learning culture in the society is supported by an equally strong teaching one. This culture of learning is also evident in the pervasive and increasing attention that school leaders pay to self-evaluation as a way to improve the school. Learning rather than measured performance defines the focus of systematic school leadership in Finnish education. Teacher quality and performance are addressed by establishing appropriate conditions to attract high level professionals through clear purpose, status, autonomy and reward. Leadership for learning, leadership by learning and leadership as learning build the culture of trust, cooperation and responsibility. At the heart of human relationships that comprise Finland's educational system are accountability and responsibility. There is a deep concern for the welfare of students and the larger community within the Finnish society. Relationships are not hierarchical but are built on the foundation of transparency—and self-evaluation remains the bedrock of leadership.

Finally, to build a culture of sustained learning, unflinching commitment is required. Schools need to focus on what author and professor of education and administration Thomas J. Sergiovanni termed as 'life-world of the school'. It focuses on the establishment of norms, values and beliefs of a school for educating the whole child. Finland, as the OECD report suggests, is a large-scale example of an experiment in educational performance. Leadership contributes to Finland's high performance not only by concentrating narrowly on performance outcomes, particularly measurable ones, but also by paying attention to the conditions, processes and goals that produce sustainable performances. Schools are bound by a common mission, a bold but unobtrusive steering system, strong governmental focus on educational development and the principals who teach themselves. This lends them credibility among the teachers and parents, enables them to remain connected with the students and ensures that pedagogical leadership is not merely rhetoric but a day-to-day reality. No wonder then, principals and teachers are regarded in Finland as a 'society of experts'.

Motion leadership recognizes that relationships matter so much that little can be accomplished without establishing trust. When the leader becomes the leading learner, willing to build all-round capacity with trust and transparency, enhanced by consistent communication throughout the process, the result is a fast-moving school heading towards the shared goals of excellence.

# 14

# Emotional Intelligence and Empathy as Tools to Promote Change

Reviews of early leadership studies in the decades of 1980s and 1990s found that intelligence did contribute to success in leadership and that academic intelligence correlated well with positive perceptions of leaders. However, the opponents of the intelligence quotient (IQ) approach claimed an overemphasis on the role of general academic intelligence in predicting leadership success. Current research studies have moved away from IQ scores as the only measure of intelligence.

As early as 1920, American psychologist Edward Lee Thorndike hypothesized that true intelligence was composed of not only the academic component but also the emotional and social components. In 1997, psychologist Reuven Bar-On argued that emotional intelligence was a much better predictor of success in life. The multiple intelligence theory of American psychologist Howard Gardener encompassed three types of mental abilities—analytical intelligence, creative intelligence and practical intelligence. Identified by psychometrician Robert Sternberg in 1985, the emotional intelligence theory later got more popularized by renowned psychologist David Goleman's writings on emotional intelligence. Goleman claimed that without emotional intelligence, the best of analytic minds, endless supply of smart ideas and the finest of training in the world will not be able to make a great leader. He articulates that leaders with emotional intelligence can arouse enthusiasm for a shared vision.

The ability to convey emotions convincingly is what separates a charismatic leader from an ordinary leader. In 2011, psychologists John Mayer, Peter Salovey, David Caruso and Lillia Cherkasskiy suggested that the ability to monitor one's own and others' feelings and emotions to discriminate among them and use it as a guide to one's own thinking and actions contributes to positive perceptions of leadership.

Skills such as flexibility, conflict management, persuasion and social reasoning have become more important to climb the ladder of success, since they can influence one's ability to succeed in coping with environmental demands and pressures. Bar-On divided emotional intelligence into five major components—intrapersonal, interpersonal, adaptability, stress management and general mood. The intrapersonal scale measured how much an individual is in touch with their own feelings and feels positive about the ways things move in their lives, while the interpersonal scale measures how well people interact and relate with each other.

Adaptability is a sign of how people are able to cope with environmental demands and pressures. Stress management reflects how people handle stress and their general mood—it is an indicator of an individual's ability to enjoy life. Organizational psychologists Barbara Mandell and Shilpa Pherwani conducted a research project to determine the leadership style of 32 managers, using the Bar-On Emotional Quotient Inventory (EQ-i) which had the above-mentioned components. Their findings convey a significant linear relationship between emotional intelligence and the transformational leadership style and how such a positive correlation can benefit an organization in several ways. Knowledge of this relationship can help organizations to identify and train potential leaders.

Today's society is faced with many challenges that require exceptional leadership, by leaders ready to lead through emotional intelligence. The educational leader required today is the one who can get beneath the surface and leverage deep change for the better. Many leadership models posit that there are two types of leaders—task and relationship leaders or socio-emotional leaders. Task leaders handle tasks that are primarily cognitive in nature, such as planning and organization, while relationship leaders continue to build high levels of motivation for organizational members.

A commonly accepted stereotypical imagination is that task leaders wear serious expressions and are too focused on emotional management traits related to delay of gratification and self-motivation. In contrast, socio-emotional leaders may wear friendly expressions, emphasizing emotions related to empathy, which is an important trait for leaders who manage their group members' emotions, particularly with regard to those related to optimism and frustration (Fig. 14). A substantial part of what sets high performers apart from peers with similar technical skills and knowledge is emotional intelligence, which is defined as the ability to understand and manage their own emotions as well as recognize and influence those of others.

Empathy, which is the ability to comprehend another's feelings and to re-experience them oneself, is a central

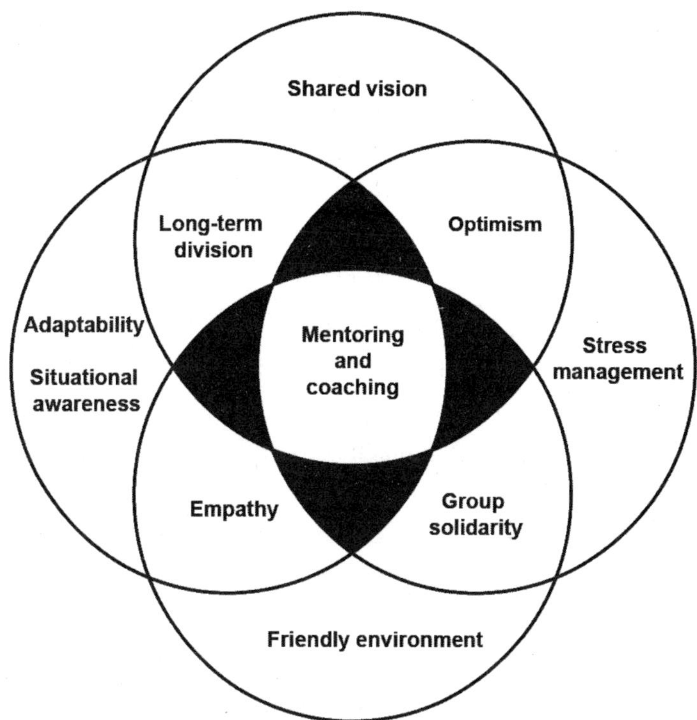


**Fig. 14: Emotional Leadership**

characteristic of emotional intelligence. It is a good indicator of the leadership's perspective, taking necessary steps for problem-solving. To analyse, discern and consider the merits of another's point of view contributes to relationship building in an organization. The ability to manage one's sense of equanimity is important for task leaders who must delay gratification while working long hours, overcome their frustrations while encountering problems, maintain confidence when facing difficult goals and marshal enthusiasm for completing the given task.

Consequent to schools going virtual for teaching, the training programmes organized for teachers also turned to online mode. The total number of teachers for this annual programme held after the summer vacation was 500 plus. These teachers were spread geographically over the entire Delhi–NCR region. From identifying the resource people to selection of the topics, extending technical help, deciding timings of training programmes to schedule 150 sessions during a period of two weeks was a mammoth task in the online format. However, the teacher who was working with me in the training department, took the entire planning, structuring and scheduling upon herself. The task involved a monumental effort since teachers themselves had to conduct this peer-to-peer training.

Guidelines were prepared and sent to all teachers for any further suggestion or modification. Zoom links were created for these sessions, formats delineated and reports uploaded to the Cloud. For every session, there was an online feedback form to be filled up by the participants. It was commendable for the training in charge along with the vice principal to make this humungous exercise possible with great success.

The vice principal who worked on the project with a lot of commitment was already working on another important school assignment which required unusually long hours of work. However, her motivation and never-say-die attitude showed through the entire task. There were occasions when gaps came into the planning owing to the virtual format—at times they didn't receive the information solicited in time but in spite of all these hurdles when finally the programme concluded after two weeks, there were only accolades from everyone. It was highly commendable how these two people maintained their zeal and equanimity throughout the period, treating the programme as their own personal mission.

In times of crisis in an organization, transformational leaders need strong emotional self-management in order to persevere under difficult circumstances. They grasp the key elements and develop a plan—the vision—that they transmit to their followers. One of the key duties of leaders is to manage the emotions of group members, to maintain optimistic mood at all times. By convincing the group members that the goals are attainable, they are able to instil a sense of confidence among them. There are times when the feelings of frustration run high in the organization. This is when emotional leaders can use their soothing affective tone to overcome the negative effects of the prevailing climate.

The last school where I worked never had any teacher union, which often grinds school to a halt with its non-cooperative stand. However, as a new principal three years back, I had to face a challenge in the election process of teachers to act as representatives of the staff. The school always had a precedence of selecting two teachers unanimously with widespread consensus after deliberations.

But it was clear this time that they were getting divided into camps for their personal vested interests. I had to get into a mess that was slowly unfolding among the staff owing to a change of leadership at every level, the chairman's, the manager's and the principal's.

I called a meeting and let everyone speak freely about why there was no consensus in the selection process. At times, it even came to squabbles among teachers. Finally, I rose to speak and gradually struck an emotional chord with everyone, reminding them of the glorious history of the educational institution. I prompted them to think why teachers never leave this school and why it is respected so much in the educational society. Would they give up everything for parochial self goals? Would they undo the legacy of the founding father of the school? Would they not like to stay as the most dedicated members of the fraternity who believed in the school vision? After an emotional appeal, I nudged them to select their representatives like every year and left the meeting. The same evening, I got a message that the teachers had agreed to have consensually selected staff representatives. Therefore, during times of ambiguity, leaders have to develop an interpretation of the emotional response that best matches the group's needs by moulding appropriate emotions. They must strive for increasing group solidarity and morale. Slowly, emotional contagion spreads from leaders to followers.

A study conducted by Michael J. Newcombe and Neal M. Ashkanasy, Australian academics of the UQ Business School, University of Queensland, in 2002 tested whether facial expressions influence our perceptions of leaders. In this study, 537 participants watched videotapes in which leaders gave either positive or negative feedback to a subordinate. Leaders who faced positive feedback but with negative facial expressions were rated lower than those who gave negative feedback with negative expressions. People often observe body language and facial expressions as clues to people's real feelings. For example, someone who praises us but, to the contrary, shows signs of actually feeling negative emotions is likely to be seen as hypocritical and insincere.

Leadership is an intrinsically emotional process, where leaders display and evoke emotions in their members. Clearly, leaders who are high in emotional intelligence would be better able to manage the impressions they give to others. Likewise, followers high in emotional intelligence would be able to detect deception better. We can envision a difficult school day for the principal, a day when he/she faces a common occurrence—for instance, finding that some teachers are late for school, which requires urgent measures to manage the smooth running of their classes at short notice. In addition, there could be a minor accident in the science lab where a student has got hurt or expensive equipment has got broken and the school nurse is frantically defending the science teacher in front of the parents. Parents who would like to settle scores with a strict teacher may use this opportunity to get back at her. But the nurse I am talking about, told the parents why there had been no serious hurt in absolutely clear medical terms. Unless the child picks up the heated equipment on his own, defying the laboratory rules, no burns can happen. Clearly, she never lost her nerve even before the most aggressive parents, who could not see any fault with their own child.

There could be another urgent issue of dealing with indiscipline in a senior class. When religious fanaticism in the country was at its peak, thanks to parochial mindsets of some politicians, some senior students also got misled into the chaotic fervour prevailing in the country. Suddenly, one day many classrooms displayed religious symbols and flags hoisted in them when teachers reached in the morning. None of the students revealed the names and there was a clear-cut solidarity visible among them. However, the students from the minority community started feeling insecure and the school being secular in nature had to dissuade students to follow fanatic ideas. Since the school had a well-established student council, the issue was finally resolved. There are times when school leaders must address student unrest through the students themselves.

Another common feature of a school day is that just when the principal is going from one crisis to another, a teacher walks in, unaware of what has happened in the school. The teacher may have scheduled a meeting for discussing the curriculum, but when she enters, the principal is already feeling very stressed and irritable. Even when the principal forces a smile to welcome the teacher, who is one of the most competent team members, and says how appreciative she is of her work, her facial expressions belie her emotions. The teacher may feel disappointed with the principal's expressions and body language, since she is not aware of what the principal experienced in the preceding hours.

In this type of situation, unless the principal is emotionally strong and able to manage her emotions to deal with the task in hand, she would not be able to make the desirable connection with the team member—a bad day in school life could result in an undesirable disruption of the relationship the principal had assiduously built with the team members over the years, if she cannot keep a rein on her emotions. Emotional leadership thus is a double-edged sword. Positive emotions can lead to a win-win situation while negative emotions could demolish the bridges of trust already built in the school.

Schools work with a multigenerational workforce, ranging from senior teachers with tenures spanning two or more decades to the young millennials. Teachers of an older generation could be loyal, with a long-term view of life, stable and less sceptical in attitude but generally less upbeat on new innovations. As opposed to this is the generation of teachers fresh from college, with clear career goals and expectations. They prefer an autonomous style of working as they are fiercely independent. Different family and social conditions which prevailed while they were growing up lend them different attributes, millennials being technically competent and result-oriented with an important need for the work–life balance.

Besides generational differences, school leaders also have to be cognisant of teachers who are less engaged with work as opposed to those who are fully committed to teaching and related tasks. In such a climate of diversity of attributes and attitudes, the principal has to deftly navigate their emotions to steer them towards organizational goals. Emotional leaders not only recognize their own emotions well but also the needs of their group members. Clearly, leaders need to have many leading styles in their repertoire to be able to switch from one to another according to the perceived trait of an individual and the prevailing situation.

The emotional intelligence framework outlined by Goleman in 2002 identifies six leadership styles based on a leader's EQ. Four of them are in the resonant style—visionary, coaching, afflictive and democratic—and have been found to have a positive impact on the organizational climate. The two dissonant styles are pacesetting and commanding, which, when used incorrectly, can cause negative impacts. In a visionary style, the leader's primary objective is to provide a long-term direction to followers who have the freedom to choose their own way of achieving it. In the coaching style, the leader works for the professional development of subordinates, which helps in building long-term capabilities. An afflictive style creates harmony among subordinates and the leader, motivating them during stressful times or for strengthening connections. The democratic style is appropriate for building a consensus in the organization after gaining valuable inputs from everyone. As for the dissonant styles, the pacesetting style accomplishes tasks to a high standard of excellence from motivated individuals, while the commanding style's primary objective is the immediate compliance of subordinates. It is common to find these styles prevailing in different schools and sometimes within the same school at different levels.

Leadership is fundamentally an emotion-management process of all the stakeholders of the organization. At a time when the world is experiencing unprecedented challenges from the Covid-19 pandemic, many organization leaders have failed to provide emotional support to team members. This period was the perfect time for leaders to go beyond their own parochial and personal tribulations, to be present for every organizational member in providing the much-needed succour. With an ailing parent at home and the Covid-19 pandemic widespread everywhere, I never forgot my responsibilities as the school leader. The entire team turned to me for emotional succour. There were teachers whose family members were stricken with the virus, some of them hospitalized in a precarious condition. From organizing everyday groceries and essentials, sending packed food to their homes, organizing whatever help they needed for transport, I stood with them throughout this period. Calling up teachers to check on their family's well-being and extending help was done every single day till everyone was back on their feet once again. From such a crisis emerged a stronger team, more cohesive and more interrelated. We heard that the leadership from the country, or institutions for that matter, often went missing, unable to assuage the followers' anxieties and uncertainties, and in the process, clearly lost their support.

The leader's behaviour can evoke a wide spectrum of emotions in followers, ranging from optimism and joy to frustration and anger, and these emotions strongly influence the overall work experience in the organization. The ability to respond empathetically and to use emotional knowledge to promote the intellectual growth of teachers is one of the most important functions of school leadership. Great leaders speak of strategy, vision and innovations but work through the emotions of all stakeholders. It is for leaders to decide whether emotions get in their way or get them on their way to glory.

# 15

# Harnessing Nuances to Bring Lasting Change

Numerous studies have affirmed the pivotal role of the school leader as a key factor in school effectiveness and as a change agent. Educational leaders are expected to develop learning communities, build the professional capacity of teachers, take advice from parents, engage in collaborative and consultative discussions, resolve conflicts, engage in instructional leadership and attend respectfully to the needs of students coming from diverse cultural, ethnic and socioeconomic backgrounds. However, surprisingly little interest is shown in leadership development. The subject is not only underresearched but also underexamined. Few countries outside of Western democracies have paid close attention to the systematic development of school leaders and the concept of actually leading rather than administering schools. We have long since moved over management now and reached the realm of leadership. Understanding nuance is a powerful call for a more evolved leadership, one that rejects short-term quick-fixes, oppositional thinking and superficial innovations with no lasting impact. Nuanced leaders go deeper than the surface to learn how things work in order to help themselves and others to figure out how to improve their functioning. They are able to mobilize organizational members to bring about a whole system change by bringing sensitivity to the context and rejecting superficiality, delving below the surface to detect patterns and their consequences to the system.

As the complexity increases, leaders have to get their messages across in an increasingly clearer way, but not by getting directly louder and emphatic—it is only by cultivating nuance. Conventional schooling is no longer able to confront the challenges that face learners in the 21st century. Not all decisions in schools require nuances, some only need decisive action. For instance, when there is a clear-cut case of flouting the school norms, then the only thing that needs to be done is to take action against the concerned person, a teacher or a student. Some matters like violence—mental or physical—use of abusive language, financial impropriety and neglect of school duties by teachers are non-negotiable acts. But anything that requires judgement, getting people on board, drawing on local knowledge, ingenuity, commitment, to name just a few, require leadership that gets beneath the surface of the problem to solve it through the process of discernment.

As the society around us keeps getting relentlessly unequal, the result is more stress, less trust, poor health and erosion of social cohesion. Eventually, greater inequality adversely affects the people throughout the organization since schools are reflections of the larger society. We are at a vital watershed moment of our times and education has to keep up with the changing times. Leadership is the key today to steer educational organizations through this fast-changing scenario. Leaders not only have to know how to get to the desired destinations but also when to change routes.

We can find leaders today who have inspired ideas but have failed to execute them. Some people who succeed marvellously while targeting change, but others using the same model may fail miserably. Some work very hard but get nowhere compared to another person who puts in half the time but gets twice as far. The difference is only in approaches. Nuanced meaning is not sought from oneself but from the people we are surrounded by. Once that learning is achieved, it stays in place. At the surface, every school leader is doing the right thing, conveying a vision, motivating students, raising teacher standards, considering student data for improvement, building professional learning communities, and so on. Yet, they achieve things differently. Some leaders work superficially as 'surfacers' while others look for principles that guide the actions which can yield results. They are 'nuancers'. They keep adjusting their actions in accordance with the changing environment.

Since my school thrives on appreciation and validation of good work, there are incidents, though rare, when teachers take such things for granted. Those who have continued without working sincerely for years on, only get more lackadaisical with this appreciation culture. Too much of democracy is often not understood in letter and spirit by some people who take it as liberty without accountability.

In such cases, teachers have to be gently reminded that institutions are larger than personal egos, and school work must always get priority while one is at work. How does one get that nuance? Can it be learnt? Is it a conceptual or practical skill? What kind of strategy is required to achieve it? Isn't nuance called for at each turn in the leader's daily interactions? The immersive and reflective thoughts for each action lay the foundation of nuance. As Michael Fullan says, 'If you have to define it, you don't have it.' To be able to see the big picture for the organization is very important for developing the nuanced approach.

Nuance which is subtle comes from the detailed observation of a phenomenon or action. Nuanced leaders work with individuals and groups in such a way that they help them develop personal meaning and collective identity to reach a goal. Such leaders have a lasting influence, beyond their tenure of leadership. These leaders see and comprehend hidden patterns and find new pathways to alter their course and shape better outcomes. They have a burning desire to make things better for everyone against all odds, remaining curious and persistent in searching for possibilities for which they detect patterns. They don't just lead, they teach. Their true success lies in their penchant for changing people's emotions, not just their minds. They build accountability in the system in such a way that every organizational member working with them sets his/her own benchmark to reach. These leaders only keep getting better with time because each effort and subsequent action make for new learning for them—a learning that endures.

When the leaders see a situation in totality, the interrelation of its various parts and the evolving situation, they learn better. That is why nuanced leaders are students first. They are willing to find answers, instead of giving them as and when required. Thus, they are reflective practitioners. They continue to connect beliefs, behaviour and consequences to work for an integrated solution. Most of all, they question their own perspective explicitly.

A research project was conducted in Victoria, Australia to study why principals' well-being was declining with increasing levels of stress and illness. The findings of the study indicated that principals believed they should be all things to all people, but this perception of the expectation of others stressed them out. Their own health and well-being was sidelined in their anxiety to avoid being evaluated negatively by their superiors and colleagues. Besides, their trust levels regarding teachers were low as they believed that unless supervised, teachers would not work for the desired objectives.

What they failed to see was that their own well-being could bring in more efficacy in their work. They had to work to change the underlying beliefs and develop those which could yield the desired outcomes. They had to start recognizing that there were alternative ways of thinking, acting and being the leader as a principal. New behaviours had to be learnt and adapted, which significantly reduced stress levels in more lasting ways. These leaders examined and questioned their own theories of action to find sustainable solutions. Principals who are learners, influence student learning explicitly. They know intuitively when to push and when to hold back, when to respond gently and when to cultivate momentum. Their distinguishing trait is that they care!

Recently, we established an open air gym in the school for teachers and students to encourage them to exercise. During the pandemic when all classes were taken from home and outside movement was curtailed for everyone, it was very clearly visible that most teachers had grown overweight. When their attention was drawn towards the health issue, they felt that it was body shaming, instead of looking at obesity as a health threat in the long run. Clearly, something had to be done. When teachers saw the state-of-the-art gym within the school premises and the principal using it herself, it was a nudge for them to act likewise. Many were reluctant earlier, but slowly the exercise regimen caught up with everyone. A physically active school is definitely a happier place.

Nuanced leaders unlock, mobilize and create a collective identity. They never become experts or specialists since they are always learning. To them, people are first (students and teachers, alike). They help their teachers to build the capacity of the students who are not doing well by identifying the impediments and promoting the conditions which can make them learn. They not only walk the talk but also talk the walk, that is, they can articulate the strategies that can improve results and get everyone to support them. Changing cultures is nuanced work because it is a process of subtly and persistently discussing and coalescing new details. Most school leaders take responsibility for several diverse tasks in a typical day, each one calling for a different way of approach. A principal could be supervising a project for science to evaluate it, followed by meetings with teachers who have departmental or interpersonal conflicts, then need to change to a totally different focus on, say, a group of non-fee paying parents, not to speak of, perhaps, a case of misdemeanour by a student lined up for the same day.

Let me quote an example here. Two senior teachers of the Hindi department have always been at loggerheads for some reason. I came to know this soon after joining the school since they often came to me, complaining about each other. It was time consuming to keep listening to their woes day after day, which incidentally had been going on for years. Departmental work was also suffering owing to this interpersonal conflict. The school teachers and authorities had already given up on them, but I knew something had to be done about it. Since they were both similarly experienced, with only some age difference between them, I decided to give the headship of the department to them on rotation. They found it uncomfortable and even unacceptable initially, but soon learnt that they had to get along with each other since they would be leading the department in alternate years, and synergy would have to be built. It started with building a working relationship first, from no communication to some communication, and the transition started happening. They also collaborated later on a project which brought in some change in their attitude towards each other. I never felt that there was any need to directly intervene in their petty squabbles as a referee, which they had initially expected from me.

That begs a question: how does the principal seamlessly move from a motivational talk to a group of students to a programme where teachers and parents have gathered to celebrate a great success in a state science exhibition or for helping teachers resolve their conflicts with each other, without shifting mental and emotional gears? The skills and values needed for different tasks of the day require adaptability since competing values involve behaviours that are opposites, such as controlling versus empowering. When their teachers have roles that are highly marked by ambiguity, nuanced leaders clarify objectives, priorities, standards and policies, providing helpful feedback and coaching. In the case mentioned above, the two teachers' strengths were identified. I often discussed their writing prowess with them, raising their self-esteem besides reminding them about the school expectations. Also, instead of offering any readymade solution to their personal differences, every time they came to me—separately—I diverted their attention to the good work they were doing, including the poetry writing they were capable of. When people start focusing on what they can do exceptionally well, they often start ignoring what they may not like or approve of. I have always believed that life doesn't get easier or more forgiving; we only get stronger and more resilient.

Jal Mehta, professor of education in the Harvard Graduate School of Education, in his work *The Allure of Order* reviews why instruments of control to achieve performance results do not work. One of the reasons why 'No Child Left Behind in the USA' failed miserably in the toughest schools is because teaching even extensively, but with external pressure, doesn't yield any worthwhile result unless students are taught in an engaging manner. To focus on learning outcomes with mechanized teaching for students subjected to long hours of studying is a lopsided view. Mutual distrust between teachers and students, between the principal and teachers on the path to improve the school is only a far-fetched strategy which leads to a downward spiral. Traditional accountability systems do not work. What is required is the cultural context and context-based accountability. No amount of external accountability will be effective in the absence of internal accountability.

—∞—

Nuanced leaders are adept at crisis management by learning to recognize early warning signs of an impending crisis instead of avoiding the common tendency to ignore or discount these signs. They not only make a quick and systematic analysis to act confidently and decisively but also remain receptive to information as it keeps evolving. They conduct a review session after a crisis ends to determine what was done well, what mistakes were made and what lessons were learnt. In short, nuanced leaders also seek insights from not so obvious places—every experience for them is a learning lesson, wherein they subject their own values and principles to a reality test. They continue to refine themselves and shift course with organizational circumstances. Though they are confident enough to be experts about what they know well, they are also humble enough to be apprentices when they need to learn from others.

As technological advancements continue at a rapid pace, each leader is expected to be in sync with what kind of technical tools are being used in the school to be able to give a genuine feedback to students. I recognized one of my weak areas very soon as the school took a giant technological leap during the pandemic. The IT department had three teachers and I requested them to take turns to train me on the new applications and tools that teachers were using. As they began their lessons with me, they not only felt very proud of themselves but also highly motivated. Soon the word spread around the school that the principal was undergoing training and just as all teachers being trained are expected to show tangible learning outcomes, I too worked on these lessons diligently. Some practice work was done every day to be able to demonstrate what I had learnt from them. When one of them quipped mischievously that they were 'mentoring the mentor', I could see how important she felt. As a lifelong learner, I was able to walk the talk with teachers because of my willingness to learn new things. What I had been saying in the staff meetings—always remain open to learn new things to grow continually—was no longer a quote but a practice visible to everyone. It was not necessarily articulated, like nuances are.

Nuanced leaders use the group itself to change its members. When the leader works alongside teachers, participating as a learner, several things happen simultaneously. A learning climate gets created and without directly exhorting teachers to change, the leader is able to move everyone forward. More gets done in less time and the group learns to feel more responsible. Nuanced leaders are also adept at resolving dilemmas. Instead of prescribing a change, such leaders can foster precision to a certain point, after which the group voluntarily takes responsibility. As the teachers continue to work through problems, they discover new practices that work better. Precision requires process, not a checklist. It is when the whole group works through the issues at hand that it gets skilled in finding effective solutions.

In any organization, feedback has a lot of value, particularly when given with candour but with respect. It is very rare to find principals who are good at giving specific feedback with finesse. Constructive feedback clarifies expectations and helps people learn from their mistakes, building their confidence. Often, principals get complacent about giving praise when things are moving fine. But it is always important to stop and smell roses to build a nurturing culture. It's human nature to put off difficult conversations or to try to soften the blow when a tough feedback is to be given. However, when the organization has a strong feedback culture in its day-to-day functioning, it helps in reinforcing positive behaviour and checking negativity.

This kind of culture is built over time by nuanced leaders. Picking the right time and place to give feedback, soon after a behavioural incident or event has happened, is very important. Specificity along with evidences to corroborate it makes for a trusting climate. Nuanced leaders do not believe followers have to first earn trust. Instead, investing in people on a daily basis is a sine qua non of such leaders. Trust is not a noun but a verb, it is a state of being. When everything is to be verified, there's no trust. I have always maintained that if the principal has to check whether teachers are taking classes punctually, then clearly, there is no trust in the system. Strong surveillance is not required to build capacity and trust. Leaders who are part and parcel of the learning process are far more successful in building trust. The built-in accountability carries the organization forward.

Haven't we all come across leaders who have an uncanny ability to see and interpret more than others can? Those who keep getting better at understanding people and cultivating cultures of accountability, keep developing their extraordinary ability at being nuanced. Frequent, continuous and transparent interaction keep building accountability. It is all about accepting the moral imperative of providing conditions of continuous growth to both teachers and students (Fig. 15). The tools of accountability

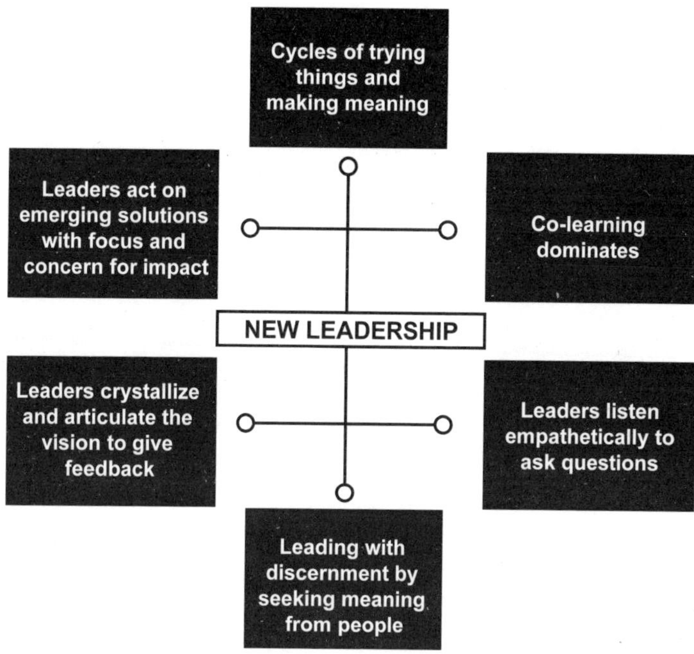


**Fig.15: Nuanced Leadership**

are not the instruments to be wielded but cultures to be built assiduously. Such a culture will automatically jettison weak practices and adopt stronger ones. Nuanced leaders gradually discover practices, usually with the people in the same situation, promising pathways to better solutions geared to what they want to accomplish. They end up developing incredibly accountable organizations because they courageously and relentlessly commit themselves to changing the system for the betterment of humanity.

# 16

# The Moral Imperative as a Driving Force

An oft-given piece of advice from educational consultants is that real leaders concentrate on doing the right thing, not on doing things right. School leaders face ethical dilemmas every day since they have moral obligations to society, to the profession, to the school board of governors, teachers, students and their parents. Schools are designed as moral institutions by default and principals are moral agents who must make decisions that favour one moral value over another. Although schools are dedicated to the well-being of children, students have virtually no voice in what happens there. Teaching the young has moral dimensions because education develops values and sensibilities as well as skills to prepare for life. For this reason, more than any, the principal's conduct must be deliberately moral. Teachers must be convinced that the principal's point of view reflects the values they support. Dilemmas arise when cherished values come into conflict. A principal who values both the teachers' autonomy and student achievement will face a dilemma when teachers want to enact a policy that lowers the bar of achievement. Many a time, principals take the path of the least resistance, by deferring to the superiors instead of doing what must be done. Principals who avoid conflict in the face of poor performances by teachers and tolerate incompetence lose the trust of every stakeholder.

Mere articulation of vision and empty rhetoric will not do anything, unless bold measures for reforms are taken. Truly effective schools are those with a shared covenant, clearly articulating the school's core values and providing a standard by which actions will be judged. Leaders must not only take the lead in formulating the covenant but also actively support and enforce it. Teachers, parents and students are all able to see through a low-key approach and, therefore, do not commit themselves to it. To mobilize all stakeholders and raising the bar is the real moral purpose. As Sergiovanni says, when a non-negotiable standard is ignored, principals must 'lead by outrage'. Moral leaders embody the message they advocate; they teach, not just through words but through actions.

It is important to remember that unless restrained by morals, the power vested with the principal is easily misused. Stewardship, which is the willingness to accept accountability for results without trying to impose control over others, gets leaders to be mindful of their own limitations. Sergiovanni, among others, argued that rationality, logic, objectivity, explicitness, individuality and detachment will take you only so far. Instead, emotions, group collegiality, sense making, duty and obligation should be the guiding forces for moral leadership. People rarely change through the rational process of Analyse-Think-Change. They are more likely to change in a See-Feel-Change context. The role of the leader is to make them see the new possibilities, see those possibilities turning into opportunities and then changing into tangible realities. Social cohesion is the need of the hour when more and more diverse learners are coming together in schools. It is not just the academic achievement that is the core function of schooling but also the personal and social development of both teachers and students. How the leader generates passion, purpose and perseverance for them is of key importance. Every school must have a solid moral purpose as a foundation. It takes commitment to further build capacity which the school leaders foster by being deeply motivated. Those who don't have the commitment and moral purpose will squander away all the resources available to them (Fig. 16).

There are numerous instances in which school leaders and teachers are called on to make decisions that have moral implications. For example, a school may have to decide whether a student must be suspended from lessons or not after displaying disruptive behaviour in the school. The school, considering its obligation to improve the behaviour of the student, may take a stand on the issue. On the one hand, the student is expected to learn from mistakes and improve. On the other, the school does not always achieve this outcome because in many cases, students may not even feel that the punishment will do them any good. Now the school has to judge whether the decision to suspend the student will benefit him. In this case, there is also a need to work out a relationship with the student so that he is able

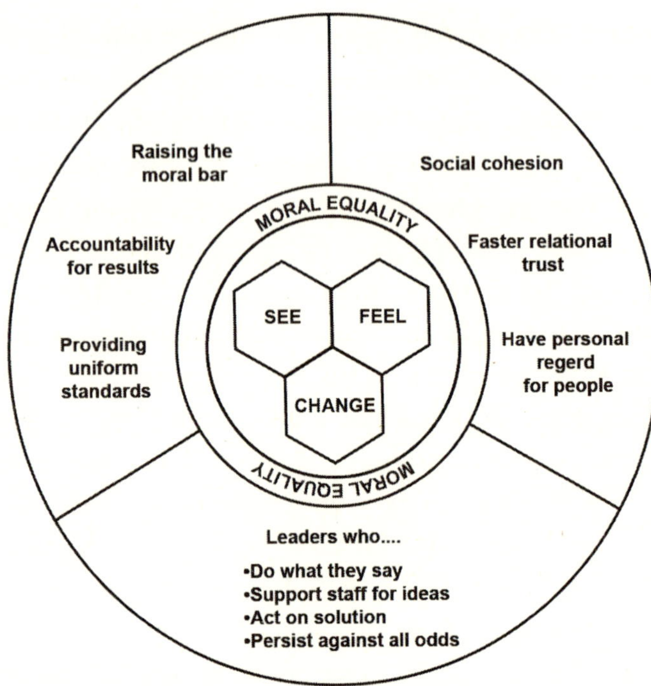


**Fig. 16: Moral Imperative For Leadership**

to see his mistakes more readily and work upon them to improve his behaviour. This will happen only when there is a climate of trust in the school.

A study, carried out by American education experts Anthony S. Bryk and Barbara Schneider in 2000, mentions about a principal who says that students are his first priority. He articulates his viewpoint by saying that trust is built by contact, by consistency, by doing what you are saying, by showing concern and by acting on solution. For him, developing trust in every operation and function in the school is of greatest importance. No wonder, when principals do not follow up on what they say, teachers lose trust in them. This is not only unprofessional behaviour but also erodes all relationships in the school. Principals drive improvement by persisting against all odds, supporting staff for their ideas, celebrating success and dealing with daily problems. They may even use problems as opportunities to reinforce school values. Such principals continually step into the unknown and encourage staff to do likewise.

Every education system needs principals who develop more leaders, thereby strengthening the school beyond themselves. Relational trust creates this moral resource. When principals and teachers hold high levels of trust, they are more willing to put in extra efforts. Bryk and Schneider identified four dimensions on which they based relational trust. These are: respect, competence, personal regard for others and integrity. These traits reflect in the day-to-day behaviour of more effective principals. The entire culture of the school with respect to teacher-principal, principal-parent, teacher-parent, teacher-teacher relations, and also how these groups relate to students' learning outcomes can be seen through the prism of the moral imperative. A serious compromise of any one criterion can be sufficient to undermine a discernment of trust in the school.

Everything cannot change only from the top. School leadership can provide vision, policies, mechanisms for coordination and collaboration but to realize these goals, there must be lateral development of leadership. The moral imperative becomes a collective endeavour only with capacity building and shared commitment. Everyone must be able to see the big picture because system-wide improvement can happen only when great ideas come from people working together.

Changing contexts of the educational field, which is most dynamic today, calls for sophisticated leadership, deeply entrenched in the moral imperative of education. A 2000 report of the OECD pertaining to assessments of PISA performances shows that two students of the same family going to different schools, one with a higher socioeconomic profile and the other with a lower one, could expect to be further apart in reading ability as compared with two students from different socioeconomic backgrounds going to the same school. This shows the value of context which is far more important than the background or personalities that people bring to a situation. Today, when we need to create a community of learners in schools, where every member feels expressed, nurtured and encouraged, the need for understanding the context cannot be overemphasized.

—~—

Strong leadership is valued by teachers for the support they need. However, what such a leadership has to be mindful about is the precondition that teachers must not feel stressed out by continuous pressures to deliver on unrealistic expectations. Moral leadership is truly enabling as it follows an incremental reform trajectory rather than pushing the agenda roughshod on teachers. Providing resources and opportunities for capacity building must precede the overall reforms. When Harvard professors and leadership authorities Ronald Heifetz and Marty Linsky concluded that effective leaders have the capacity to be on the dance floor as well as the balcony simultaneously, they clearly alluded to leaders who operate at all levels. The more principals know about one level, the more they will be able to influence at other levels. A climate of relationship trust develops in daily social exchanges and grows over time. An ethos of trust develops when leaders do not engage in arbitrary actions. A genuine professional community of teachers emerges when principals lead from the front and reach out to others. They can develop competence trust in the school by respecting teachers' knowledge, skills and abilities. Contractual trust can be developed by managing expectations and establishing boundaries. Communication trust develops by sharing information, admitting and learning from mistakes as well as maintaining confidentiality, as emphasized by Dennis S. Reina and Michelle L. Reina, specialists in trust building in workplaces, in their 1999 book, *Trust and Betrayal in the Workplace*.

Some of the self- or system-imposed barriers to school leadership are perceived system limitations, the vicious circle of 'If Only', loss of a moral compass and inability to change one's own learning. The trap of 'If Only' kills not only the principal's motivation but also becomes a tool in the hands of incompetent teachers who fail to deliver. Principals, who only see the potential obstacles for implementing any strategy they have conceived, continue to lead passively. They often prefer to conform rather than boldly go ahead with reforms. The managerial norms of efficiency, specificity, rationality, measurability and objectivity have created a myth that good management is necessarily 'tough minded'. This has been the essence of mainstream management in the West. These capacities are, however, far from sufficient to address the complexity of life in schools. One of the greatest strengths leaders need today, especially in troubled times like the current Covid pandemic, is a strong sense of moral purpose. The fundamental reason why they are in the school education field must continue to guide them at all times. With their sights firmly on the legacy they want to leave, principals must continue to move ahead, using their moral compass. The principal has to be a lead learner, going out of her way to learn continuously.

Some school boards do not invest enough in leadership development and, worst of all, neglect the leadership succession question. What normally happens in such a case is a mindless and arbitrary placement of leaders who neither have the acumen to lead nor the ability to carry forward the legacy of an established school. School leadership is not just about the day-to-day running of the school, but long-term strategies. A system which neither regards experience and global exposure nor values people who can bring about the much-needed changes, can go only so far. Such school's management have a lot of soul-searching to do. There are also schools which have not grown to their much-deserved position even after decades in education. Pedagogical experience is not valued by them and they continue to 'operate' without an academic visionary at the helm who could take them to the next level. Such schools get left behind even by much newer entrants in the education field, in spite of starting with a noble social cause of educating the disadvantaged. An inward-looking kind of education system can never grow outwards, when education is all about extending the wings of imagination and innovation all around. Such schools need very bold reforms to be able to move out of their decades-long inertia.

Sergiovanni has defined the sources of authority for leadership in schools as Bureaucratic, Psychological, Technical-rational, Professional and Moral. Bureaucratic styles of leadership rely on mandates, rules, regulations, job descriptions, monitoring and controlling the staff and students. This kind of leadership I experienced in the first school where I joined soon after BEd. Teachers couldn't think for themselves, and students did what they were 'told'. That school, sadly, remains in the same rut even after 35 years. Needless to say, that even 35 years before I joined, it was just the same. It never had a visionary as a leader. This kind of leadership model occupies the lowest stage of moral development. Even psychological leadership, which draws its authority from motivation and human relationship skills, is transactional in nature. It focuses on control and advocates the spirit of 'what gets rewarded or punished gets done'. When leadership thrives on charisma, there are many followers who do as they are asked, believing blindly in their leaders. When they don't fall in line, they are penalized for that. Such leadership does not tap into the full depth of human capacity. Leadership is never about the leader, it's about investing in the growth of others. When we talk to leaders who hold the reins of control, we get the feeling that they are important. The point is: shouldn't we have leaders who give us a feeling that we are important?

Similarly, the technical-rational authority of leadership, which is highly prized in the modern society, does not really bring in lasting changes. The human activities of teaching-learning are too complex to be reduced to rules and procedures. When educational goals get decided by sifting through data, analysing trends, interpreting them for future design, clearly we are missing out on the crux of the leadership. Students are not just customers who are being provided with a service. Number crunching may bode well for politicians where elections have to be won. We, as school leaders, are here to raise everyone to the highest level of self-actualization. School leaders set out to make a difference to the very existence of students with their attitudes towards learning, which shapes their lives.

Much to the chagrin of my school board, I have always believed that education cannot be completely standardized, since it is neither linear nor sequential. No amount of standardized testing can judge teachers' competence and student attainment. Every year, the students of Grades 5 and 8 go through standardized testing in language and numeracy after which the results are compared with all the other schools under the aegis of the same educational trust. Thereafter, there are days of judgement passed by the chief executive officer (CEO) of the trust from his high pedestal about which school is performing and which one is languishing. This not only demoralizes the teachers of these schools but also brings in undue competition where the only yardstick for measuring ability is the marks in these tests, regardless of what else the students have achieved. If it were about a product where every single piece had to undergo strict quality testing, before being sent to the market, it would have been acceptable. But schools are not factories and leaders are not quality inspectors. They are educationists and the highest level of leadership is to be found in moral and ethical domains. The moral purpose of the highest order is like having a system where all students learn, the gap between high and low performers being steadily reduced. Teachers grow every day and leaders take the entire community towards the highest levels of abilities and competence.

An important question to be asked by the principal is: what is my role in making a difference in the school as a whole? Unless all educational goals are achieved and the culture of the school becomes so transformed that the entire school learns continuously, the moral imperative is not achieved. Moral leadership focuses directly on articulating and upholding important school values. It can leave a lasting impact on the life of teachers and students. This is not to say that rules, regulations and policies are to be replaced. Rather, they need to be supplemented and enriched with a moral imperative.

Schools carry with them a sense of guardianship for educating the society's youth. Education is a conscious effort to develop values, sensibilities as well as skills in the future citizenry of the world. A strong moral imperative foundation is the sine qua non of societal development and extends beyond material gain or personal achievement. By making lives better for people around, leaders must provide meaning in life. As Michael Fullan expounded in his book *The Moral Imperative of School Leadership*, the moral imperative in the hands of school leaders is our greatest hope for transforming schools.

# CONCLUSION
## Leadership Matters

Human beings are designed for learning. No one teaches an infant to walk and no child masters spatial relationships before stacking building blocks in order to ensure that they don't topple over. Children explore and experiment to keep discovering how they will navigate their daily life. Unfortunately, schools that are the primary institutions of a society are oriented predominantly towards controlling rather than learning. A young child who enters the school environment quickly discovers that the name of the game is getting the answer right and avoiding any mistake. The inherent intrinsic motivation, self-esteem, dignity, curiosity to learn and joy in learning, all take a back seat as the focus becomes performing for someone else's approval. If anything, the need for a school leader to understand how organizations learn is greater than ever before. In today's increasingly unpredictable and uncertain world, leadership has become much more subtle. Building the school culture and shaping its constant evolution need leadership roles played actively—from a designer to a teacher, from a steward to a systems thinker. The job is to navigate deftly though myriad of demands for creating a learning organization.

Scratch the surface of an excellent school and one is likely to find an excellent principal. Peer into a failing school and you will find a weak leadership. That gives a renewed emphasis on educational leadership to understand what works in leadership. However, like any other complex human activity, leadership is difficult to narrow down to a few aspects although at the core of leadership is a shared purpose and direction for which the leaders work through other people. It is more like a function than a role. As we have seen, leadership is often invested in or expected of a person in a position of formal authority. Formal leaders are genuine leaders only to the extent that they fulfil these functions. School leaders influence the stakeholders by galvanizing effort around ambitious goals and by establishing conditions that support teachers to help students succeed. Clearly, principals exert leadership through constellation of actions that coalesce around different styles of leadership.

Effective educational leaders endorse the vision that embodies the best thinking about teaching and learning. The shared purpose acts as a basic stimulant for one's work. School effectiveness is enhanced when both the leaders and the broader community share clear understandings about students, learning and schooling. To convey their expectations for quality and high performance, leaders sharpen perceptions of the gap between what the school aspires to achieve and what is being accomplished in the present. They use multiple indicators to monitor organizational performance and continue to review and develop them. This requires astute skills for gathering, interpreting and synthesizing information. They ask questions that are critical yet constructive and emphasize the use of systematic evidence. Their participatory communication style engages everyone and offers intellectual stimulation. They encourage reflection and challenge their staff to examine assumptions about their work, providing incentives and structures simultaneously to achieve necessary changes. Not only do they succeed in achieving organizational goals but also changing the mindsets of the staff by way of commitment, capacity and resilience.

To take the analogy of a school leader as the captain and the school as a ship to be steered in waters, calm or stormy, the most important task is to set the direction. No one has a greater impact on the future of the ship's voyage than the designer of the ship. If the designer, that is, the principal, has built a rudder that will only turn to port 30, then what is the point of envisioning the process of turning the starboard to 35 degrees? The social architecture of the school is very important to take it to the desired direction. The vision of the school, the tenets by which it will function, the mission it will achieve and the core values by which its stakeholders will live, are all just a few acts which will be deeply influenced by the school leadership. New leadership roles of the 21st century require new leadership skills and styles.

Building a shared vision for the entire organization requires a very clear personal vision. This vision then needs to be communicated and support asked of all people involved to reach its goals. As Steve Jobs, the co-founder of Apple, who is widely recognized as a pioneer of personal computer revolution famously said, 'If you are working on something exciting that you really care about, you don't have to be pushed. The vision pulls you.' Leadership is a never-ending process. With the changing time and tide, the vision keeps evolving. Leaders who help people see the big picture are also able to see interrelationships and patterns, not just snapshots and isolated events. They move beyond blaming a restrictive environment, incompetent people, unmotivated individuals and other factors that hinder the building of a learning organization. Instead, they believe that there is the vision or a goal encompassing nothing outside the system since everyone and their problems are a part of the single organizational whole. Their well-focused actions produce lasting and enduring improvements.

To sum this perspective up, there are many personal attributes of leadership such as loyalty, integrity, reliability, positive self-esteem and ability to deal with pressure with resilience that go a long way in building a successful leader. Schools need to grow beyond the academic and cognitive domains to the non-cognitive and social domains. Excellent school leaders remember at all times that they are building the society. Their students and teachers bring knowledge, values, preferences and dispositions to the school which turn into valuable social capital under the guidance of an excellent school leader. As Peter Drucker famously said, leadership is lifting a person's vision to high sights, the leading of a person's performance to a higher standard and the building of a personality beyond its normal limits. Educational leadership and learning are intertwined for building destiny of a nation—and excellent schools come into being through excellent principals.

# Reference List

Abbas, G., J. Iqbal, A. Waheed and M. N. Riaz. 2012. 'Relationship between Transformational Leadership Style and Innovative Work Behavior in Educational Institutions'. *Journal of Behavioral Sciences* vol. 22, no. 3: pp. 18-32.

Acker-Hocewar, M. and D. Touchton. 1999. 'A Model of Power as Social Relationships: Teacher Leaders Describe the Phenomena of Effective Agency in Practice'. Paper presented at the annual meeting of the American Educational Research Association, Montreal, Quebec, Canada.

Adeyemi, T.O. 2010. 'Principals' Leadership Styles and Teachers' Job Performance in Senior Secondary Schools in Ondo State, Nigeria'. *Journal of Education Administration and Policy Studies* vol. 2, no. 6: pp. 83-91.

Aiello, Antonio, Patrizia Deitinger, Christian Nardella and Michela Bonafede. 2008. 'A Tool for Assessing the Risk of Mobbing in Organizational Environments: The "Val. Mob." Scale'. *Prevention Today* vol. 4, no. 3: pp. 9-24.

Allison, Scott T., George R. Goethals and Roderick M. Kramer (eds). 2017. *Handbook of Heroism and Heroic Leadership*. New York: Routledge.

Antonakis, John. 2001. 'The Validity of the Transformational, Transactional and Laissez-Faire Leadership Model as

Measured by the Multifactor Leadership Questionnaire (MLQ5X)'. *Dissertation Abstracts International* vol. 62, no. 1: p. 233.

Archer, David and Alex Cameron. 2013. *Collaborative Leadership: Building Relationships, Handling Conflict and Sharing Control*, 2nd edn. New York: Routledge.

Argyris, C. 1993. *On Organisational Learning*. London: Blackwell.

Ayman, Roya. 2004. 'Situational and Contingency Approaches to Leadership'. In *The Nature of Leadership*, edited by John Antonakis, A.T. Cianciolo and Robert J. Sternberg, pp. 148-70. Thousand Oaks, CA: Sage.

Barker, R.A. 2001. 'The Nature of Leadership'. *Human Relations* vol. 54, no. 4 (April): pp. 469-94. https://doi.org/10.1177/0018726701544004.

Bar-On, Reuven. 2000. 'Emotional and Social Intelligence: Insights from the Emotional Quotient Inventory'. In *The Handbook of Emotional Intelligence*, edited by Reuven Bar-On and James D.A. Parker, pp. 363-88. San Francisco: Jossey-Bass.

Barth, Roland S. 2001. 'Teacher Leader'. *Phi Delta Kappan* vol. 82, no. 6 (February): pp. 443-49.

Bass, Bernard M. 1985. *Leadership and Performance beyond Expectations*. NY: Free Press.

Bass, Bernard M. 1997. 'Does the Transactional-Transformational Leadership Paradigm Transcend Organizational and National Boundaries?' *American Psychologist* vol. 52, no. 2: pp. 130-39.

Bass, Bernard M., Bruce J. Avolio, Dong I. Jung, Yair Berson. 2003. 'Predicting Unit Performance by Assessing Transformational and Transactional Leadership'. *Journal of Applied Psychology* vol. 88, no. 2: pp. 207-18.

Bittel, Lester R. 1964. *Management by Exception: Systematizing and Simplifying the Managerial Job*. New York: McGraw-Hill, 1964.

Blasé, Jo. and Joseph Blasé. 1999. 'Implementation of Shared Governance for Instructional Improvement: Principals' Perspective', *Journal of Educational Administration* vol. 37, no. 5 (December): pp. 476-500.

Block, Peter. 1994. *Stewardship: Choosing Service Over Self-interest.* San Francisco: Berrett-Koehler Publishers.

Bono, Joyce E., and M.H. Anderson. 2005. 'The Advice and Influence Networks of Transformational Leaders'. *Journal of Applied Psychology* vol. 90, no. 6: pp. 1306-14.

Bono, Joyce E. and Remus Ilies. 2006. 'Charisma, Positive Emotions and Mood Contagion'. *The Leadership Quarterly* vol. 17, no. 4 (August): pp. 317-34.

Bryk, Anthony S. and Barbara Schneider. 2002. *Trust in Schools: A Core Resource for Improvement.* New York: The Russell Sage Foundation.

Burns, J.M. 1978. *Leadership.* New York: Harper and Row Publishers.

Bush, Tony and Derek Glover. 2003. 'School Leadership: Concepts and Evidence'. A Review of Literature Carried out for National College for School Leadership, Nottingham (www.ncsl).

Camburn, Eric, Brian Rowan and James Taylor. 2003. 'Distributed Leadership in Schools: The Case of Elementary Schools Adopting Comprehensive School Reform Models'. *Educational Evaluation and Policy Analysis* vol. 25, no. 4: pp. 347-73.

Chapman, C. 2002. 'School Improvement in Challenging Circumstances: The Role of External Inspection'. Paper presented as part of the symposium 'School Improvement in Challenging Circumstances', ICSEI 2002 Copenhagen.

Collins, James. 1996. 'Socialization to Text: Structure and Contradiction in Schooled Literacy'. In *Natural Histories of Discourse*, edited by Michael Silverstein and Greg Urban. Chicago: University of Chicago Press.

Collins, Jim. 2001. *Good to Great.* New York: HarperCollins Publishers.

Conger, Jay A. 1990. 'The Dark Side of Leadership'. *Organizational Dynamics* vol. 19, no. 2 (Autumn): pp. 44-55.

Conger, Jay A. and Rabindra N. Kanungo. 1998. *Charismatic Leadership in Organizations.* Thousand Oaks, CA: Sage Publications.

Day, C. and A. Harris. 2002. 'Teacher Leadership, Reflective Practice and School Improvement'. In *Second International Handbook of Educational Leadership and Administration*, edited by K.A. Leithwood and P. Hallinger, pp. 957-977. Netherlands: Springer.

Day, David V. 2000. 'Leadership Development: A Review in Context', *The Leadership Quarterly* vol. 11, no. 4: pp. 581-613.

Day, David V., Peter C. Gronn and Eduardo Salas. 2004. 'Leadership Capacity in Teams'. *The Leadership Quarterly* vol. 15, no. 6: pp. 857-80.

De Cremer, David and Daan van Knippenberg. 2004. 'Leader Self-sacrifice and Leadership Effectiveness: The Moderating Role of Leader Self-confidence'. *Organizational Behavior and Human Decision Making Process* vol. 95, no. 2 (November): pp. 140-55.

Drucker, Peter F. 1954. *The Practice of Management.* New York: Harper & Row.

Drysdale, L., J.V. Bennet, E.T. Murakami and O. Johansson, 2014. 'Heroic Leadership in Australia, Sweden, and the United States'. *European Journal of Marketing* vol. 28, no. 7 (September).

Elmore, Richard F. 2000. Building a New Structure for School Leadership. Washington DC: The Albert Shanker Institute.

Elmore, Richard F. and Deanna Burney. 1999. 'Investing in Teacher Learning: Staff Development and Instructional

Improvement'. In *Teaching as a Learning Profession: Handbook of Policy and Practice*, edited by L. Darling-Hammond and G. Sykes, pp. 263-91. San Francisco: Jossey-Bass.

Fink, E. and L.B. Resnick. 2001. 'Developing Principals as Instructional Leaders'. *Phi Delta Kappan* vol. 82, no. 8.

Foels, Robert E., James E. Driskell, Brian Mullen and Eduardo Salas. 2000. 'The Effects of Democratic Leadership on Group Member Satisfaction: An Integration'. *Small Group Research* vol. 31, no. 31: pp. 676-701.

Frost, D. and J. Durrant. 2003. 'Teacher Leadership: Rationale, Strategy and Impact'. *School Leadership and Management* vol. 23, no. 2: pp. 173-186.

Fuad, D.R.S.M., K. Musa and Z. Hashim. 2020. 'A Perspective to Innovation Leadership in Malaysia Education'. *Journal of Educational Research and Indigenous Studies* vol. 1, no. 1: pp. 1-17.

Fullan, Michael. 1997. *What's Worth Fighting for in the Principalship?* (2nd edn.). New York: Teachers' College Press.

Fullan, Michael. 1999. *Change Forces: The Sequel.* London: Taylor and Francis.

Fullan, Michael. 2001. *Leading in a Culture of Change.* San Francisco: Jossey-Bass.

Fullan, Michael. 2002. 'Principals as Leaders in a Culture of Change', *Educational Leadership* Special Issue (May).

Fullan, Michael. 2003. *Change Forces with a Vengeance.* London: Falmer Press.

Fullan, Michael. 2003. *The Moral Imperative of School Leadership.* Thousand Oaks, CA: Corwin Publishing.

Fullan, Michael. 2003. *The Moral Imperative of School Leadership.* Thousand Oaks, CA: Corwin Publishing.

Fullan, Michael. 2010. *Motion Leadership: The Skinny on Becoming Change Savvy.* Thousand Oaks, California: Corwin Publishing.

Fullan, Michael. 2014. *The Principal: Three Keys to Maximizing Impact.* San Francisco, CA: Jossey-Bass.

Fullan, Michael. 2015. 'Leadership from the Middle: A System Strategy'. *Education Canada*, Canadian Education Association.

Fullan, Michael. 2018. *Nuance: Why Some Leaders Succeed and Others Fail.* Thousand Oaks, CA: Corwin Publishing.

Furman, Gali C. and Robert J. Starratt. 2002. 'Leadership for Democratic Community in Schools'. In *The Educational Leadership Challenge: Redefining Leadership for the 21st Century*, edited by J. Murphy, pp. 105-33. Chicago: University of Chicago Press.

Gardner, H.E. 1983. *Frames of Mind: The Theory of Multiple Intelligences.* New York: Basic Books.

Gardner, H.E. 1995. *Leading Minds: An Anatomy of Leadership.* New York: Basic Books.

Gladwell, Malcolm. 2000. *The Tipping Point: How Little Things Can Make a Big Difference.* Boston: Little, Brown.

Goleman, D. 2004. 'What Makes a Leader?' *Harvard Business Review* (Product R0104H).

Goleman, D. 2005. *Emotional Intelligence: Why it Can Matter More Than IQ.* London: Bantam Press.

Goleman, D., R. Boyatzis and A. McKee. 2002. *Primal Leadership: Realizing the Power of Emotional Intelligence.* Boston: Harvard Business School Press.

Goleman, D., R. Boyatzis and A. McKee. 2002. *The New Leaders: Transforming the Art of Leadership into the Science of Results.* London: Little, Brown.

Goodlad, John I., R. Soder and K. A. Sirotnik (ed). 1990. *The Moral Dimension of Teaching.* San Francisco: Jossey-Bass.

Greenfield, W.D. 1995. 'Towards a Theory of School Administration: The Centrality of Leadership'. *Educational Administration Quarterly* vol. 31, no. 1 (February): pp. 61.

Gronn, Peter C. 2003. *The New Work of Educational Leaders: Changing Leadership Practice in an Era of School Reform.* London: Paul Chapman Publications.

Gronn, Peter. 2000. 'Distributed Properties: A New Architecture for Leadership'. *Educational Management and Administration* vol. 28, no. 3 (July): pp. 317-38.

Gronn, Peter. 2008. 'The Future of Distributed Leadership'. *Journal of Educational Administration* vol. 46, no. 2: pp. 141-58.

Hairon, Salleh and Clive Dimmock. 2012. 'Singapore Schools and Professional Learning Communities: Teacher Professional Development and School Leadership in an Asian Hierarchical System', *Educational Review* (Routledge) vol. 64, no. 4: pp. 405-24.

Hallinger, P. and R.H. Heck. 2010. 'Leadership for Learning: Does Collaborative Leadership Make a Difference?' *Educational Management, Administration and Leadership* vol. 38, no. 6 (November): pp. 654-78.

Hargreaves, Andy and Michael Fullan. 2012. *Professional Capital: Transforming Teaching in Every School.* New York; London: Routledge.

Hargreaves, Andy, Alan Boyle and Alma Harris. 2014. *Uplifting Leadership: How Organizations, Teams, and Communities Raise Performance* (1st edn). San Francisco: Jossey-Bass.

Hargreaves, David H. 2003. *Education Epidemic: Transforming Secondary Schools Through Innovation Networks.* London: DEMOS.

Harris, Alma and D. Muijs. 2003. *Teacher Leadership: Principles and Practice.* UK: National College for School Leadership.

Harris, Alma and D. Muijs. 2004. *Improving Schools Through Teacher Leadership.* London: Open University Press.

Harris, Alma. 2007. 'Distributed Leadership: Conceptual Confusion and Empirical Reticence'. *International Journal of Leadership in Education* vol. 10, no. 3: pp. 1-11.

Harris, Alma. 2008. *Distributed School Leadership: Developing Tomorrow's Leaders.* London: Routledge.

Hattie, John. 2009. *Visible Learning: A Synthesis of Over 800 Meta-Analyses Relating to Achievement* (1st edn). London; New York: Routledge.

Heifetz, R.A. and M. Linsky. 2002. *Leadership on the Line: Staying Alive Through the Dangers of Leading*, Boston: Harvard Business Press.

Hofstede, Geert, Gert Jan Hofstede, Michael Minkov. 1991. *Cultures and Organizations: Software of the Mind.* New York: McGraw-Hill.

Humphrey, R.H. 2002. 'The Many Faces of Emotional Leadership'. *The Leadership Quarterly* vol. 13: pp. 493-504.

Jago, Arthur G. 1982. 'Leadership: Perspectives in Theory and Research'. *Management Science* vol. 28, no. 3 (March): pp. 315-36.

Karim, A.J. 2016. 'The Indispensable Styles, Characteristics and Skills for Charismatic Leadership in Times of Crisis'. *International Journal of Advanced Engineering, Management and Science* vol. 2, no. 5 (May): pp. 363-72.

Khalili, Ashkan. 2017. 'Creative and Innovative Leadership: Measurement Development and Validation'. *Management Research Review.* vol. 40, no. 10 (October): pp. 1117-38.

Kilicoglu, D. 2018. 'Understanding Democratic and Distributed Leadership: How Democratic Leadership of School Principals Related to Distributed Leadership in Schools? *Educational Policy Analysis and Strategic Research* vol. 13, no. 3: pp. 6-23.

Kotter, John P. and Dan S. Cohen. 2002. *The Heart of Change.* Boston: Harvard Business School Press.

Kuhn, Thomas S. 1962. *The Structure of Scientific Revolutions.* Chicago: University of Chicago Press.

Laleo lu, A. and E. Özmete. 2013. 'Mobbing Ölçe i: Geçerlik ve güvenirlik çalı ması'. *Journal of Social Policy Studies* vol. 13, no. 31: pp. 9-31.

Leithwood, K. 2001. 'School Leadership in the Context of Accountability Policies'. *International Journal of Leadership in Education*, vol. 4, no. 3: pp. 217-35.

Leithwood, K. and B. Mascall. 2007. 'Collective Leadership Effects on Student Achievement'. American Educational Research Association. Chicago, IL.

Leithwood, K., and D. Jantzi,. 2000. 'The Effects of Transformational Leadership on Organizational Conditions and Student Engagement with School'. *Journal of Educational Administration* vol. 38, no. 2 (May): pp. 112-129.

Leithwood, K. and B. Mascall. 2008. 'Collective Leadership Effects on Student Achievement'. *Educational Administration Quarterly* vol. 44, no, 4: pp. 496-528.

Leithwood, K. and Karen Seashore Louis. 2011. *Linking Leadership to Student Learning* (1st edn). San Francisco: Jossey-Bass.

Leithwood, K. and R. Steinbach. 2003. 'Successful Leadership for Especially Challenging Schools'. In *Handbook of Educational Leadership and Management*, edited by Brent Davies and John West-Burnham, pp. 25-43. London: Pearson Education.

Leithwood, K., Michael Fullan and N. Watson. 2003. 'The Schools We Need: A New Blueprint for Ontario'. Ontario: Atkinson Foundation.

Leithwood, Kenneth, Karen Seashore Louis, Stephen Anderson and Kyla Wahlstrom. 2004. 'How Leadership Influences Student Learning'. New York: The Wallace Foundation.

Lewin, Kurt, R. Lippitt and R. K. White. 1939. 'Patterns of Aggressive Behavior in Experimentally Created Social

Climates'. *The Journal of Social Psychology* vol. 10, no. 2: pp. 271-99.

Liu, Yan, Mehmet Sukru Bellibas and Susan Printy. 2018. 'How School Context and Educator Characteristics Predict Distributed Leadership: A Hierarchical Structural Equation Model with 2013 TALIS Data', *Educational Management Administration and Leadership* vol. 46, no. 3 (May): pp. 401-23.

Luthans, F. and B.J. Avolio. 2003. 'Authentic Leadership: A Positive Developmental Approach'. In *Positive Organizational Scholarship: Foundations of a New Discipline*, edited by K.S. Cameron, J.E. Dutton and R.E. Quinn, pp. 241-58. San Francisco, CA: Berrett-Koehler Publishers.

Malone, Helen Janc (ed). 2013. *Leading Educational Change: Global Issues, Challenges, and Lessons on Whole-System Reform.* New York: Teachers' College Press.

Mandell, B. and S. Pherwani, 2003. 'Relationship between Emotional Intelligence and Transformational Leadership Style: A Gender Comparison'. *Journal of Business and Psychology* vol. 17, no. 3 (March): pp. 387-404.

Maner, J.K. and N.L. Mead. 2010. 'The Essential Tension between Leadership and Power: When Leaders Sacrifice Group Goals for the Sake of Self-interest'. *Journal of Personality and Social Psychology* vol. 99, no. 3: pp. 482-97.

Marks, Helen M. and Susan M. Printy. 2003. 'Principal Leadership and School Performance: An Integration of Transformational and Instructional Leadership'. *Educational Administration Quarterly* vol. 39, no. 3 (August): pp. 370-97.

Mayer, John D., P. Salovey, D. R. Caruso and L. Cherkasskiy. 2011. 'What Is Emotional Intelligence and Why Does it Matter? In *The Cambridge Handbook of Intelligence* (third edn.), edited by R.J. Sternberg and J. Kaufman, pp. 528-49. New York: Cambridge University Press.

Mehta, J. 2013a. *The Allure of Order: High Hopes, Dashed Expectations and the Troubled Quest to Remake American Schooling*. New York: Oxford University Press.

Mintrop, H. 2003. *Schools on Probation: How Accountability Works (and Doesn't Work)*. New York: Teachers College Press.

Mitchell, C. and L. Sackney. 2000. *Profound Improvement: Building Capacity for a Learning Community*. Lisse: Swets & Zeitlinger.

Mittal, R. 2015. 'Charismatic and Transformational Leadership Styles: A Cross-cultural Perspective'. *International Journal of Business and Management* vol. 10, no. 3: pp. 26-33.

Moos, L. and S. Huber. 2007. 'School Leadership, School Effectiveness and School Improvement: Democratic and Integrative Leadership. In *International Handbook of School Effectiveness and Improvement,* edited by T. Townsend, pp. 579-96. Netherlands: Springer.

Mulford, Bill and Halia Silins. 2003. 'Leadership for Organizational Learning and Improved Student Outcomes—What Do We Know?' *Cambridge Journal of Education* vol. 33, no. 2 (July): pp. 175-95.

Mulford, Bill. 1998. 'Organisational Learning and Educational Change'. In *International Handbook of Educational Change*, edited by A. Hargreaves, A. Lieberman, M. Fullan and D.W. Hopkins, pp. 616-641. Netherlands: Springer.

Newcombe, M.J. and N.M. Ashkanasy. 2002. 'The Role of Affect and Affective Congruence in Perceptions of Leaders: An Experimental Study'. *The Leadership Quarterly* vol. 13, no. 5: pp. 601-14.

OECD. 2011. 'School Autonomy and Accountability: Are They Related to Student Performance? PISA in Focus 9'. Paris: OECD Publishing.

OECD. 2013. 'Education Policy Outlook: Finland'.

OECD. 2013. PISA 2012 Results: Excellence Through Equity, Giving Every Student the Chance to Succeed, vol. 2. Paris: OECD Publishing.

OECD. 2014. Measuring Innovation in Education: A New Perspective, Educational Research and Innovation, Paris: OECD Publishing.

OECD. 2015a. Schooling Redesigned: Towards Innovative Learning Systems, Educational Research and Innovation. Paris: OECD Publishing.

OECD. 2015b. 'Education Policy Outlook 2015: Making Reforms Happen'. Paris: OECD Publishing.

Ogawa, R.T. and S.T. Bossert. 1997. 'Leadership as an Organization Quality'. In *Leadership and Teams in Educational Management*, edited by Megan Crawford, Lesley Kydd and Colin Riches. Buckingham: Open University Press.

Ontario Ministry of Education. 2004. Support for Schools That Need Extra Help. Toronto: Ontario Ministry of Education.

Peker, Sevinç, Yusuf Inandi and Fahrettin Giliç. 2018. 'The Relationship between Leadership Styles (Autocratic and Democratic) of School Administrators and the Mobbing Teachers Suffer'. *European Journal of Contemporary Education* vol. 7, no. 1: pp. 150-64.

Price, T.L. 2004. *Ethics, the Heart of Leadership*, edited by J.B Ciulla, Upper Saddle River: Wharton School Publishing.

Reina, Dennis S. and Michelle L. Reina. 1999. *Trust and Betrayal in the Workplace: Building Effective Relationships in Your Organization*. San Francisco: Berrett-Koehler Publishers.

Robinson, Viviane M. J. 2010. 'From Instructional Leadership to Leadership Capabilities: Empirical Findings and Methodological Challenges'. *Leadership and Policy in Schools* vol. 9, no. 1 (February): pp. 1-26.

Robinson, Viviane M.J. 2001. 'Embedding Leadership in Task Performance'. In *Leadership for Quality Schooling: International Perspectives*, edited by K. Wong and C. Evers, pp. 90-102. London: Falmer Press.

Robinson, Viviane M.J. 2006. 'Putting Education Back into Educational Leadership'. *Leading and Managing* vol. 12, no. 1: pp. 62-75.

Robinson, Viviane M.J. 2008. 'Forging the Links Between Distributed Leadership and Educational Outcomes'. *Journal of Educational Administration* vol. 46, no. 2: pp. 241-56.

Senge, Peter, H. Hamilton, and J. Kania. 2015. 'The Dawn of System Leadership'. *Stanford Social Innovation Review* vol. 13: pp. 27-33.

Senge, Peter, A. Kleiner, C. Roberts, R. Ross, G. Roth, B. Smith and E. C. Guman. 1999. *The Dance of Change: The Challenges to Sustaining Momentum in Learning Organizations.* NY: Doubleday/Currency.

Senge, Peter, N. H. Cambron-McCabe, T. Lucas, B. Smith, J. Dutton and A. Kleiner. 2000. *Schools That Learn: A Fifth Discipline Fieldbook for Educators, Parents, and Everyone Who Cares About Education.* NY: Currency/Doubleday.

Senge, Peter. 2006. *The Fifth Discipline: The Art and Practice of the Learning Organization* (revised and updated edn). NY: Currency/Doubleday.

Sergiovanni, Thomas J. 1991. *The Principalship: A Reflective Practice Perspective.* Needham Heights, Massachusetts: Allyn and Bacon.

Sergiovanni, Thomas J. 1992. Moral Leadership: *Getting to the Heart of School Improvement*, San Francisco, CA: Jossey-Bass.

Sergiovanni, Thomas J. 1999. *The Lifeworld of Leadership: Creating Culture, Community, and Personal Meaning in Our Schools.* San Francisco, CA: Jossey-Bass.

Shabani, K., Khatib, M., and Ebadi, S. 2010. 'Vygotsky's zone of proximal development: Instructional implications and teachers' professional development'. *English Language Teaching* vol. 3, no. 4: pp. 237-248.

Shamir, Boas. 1991. 'The Charismatic Relationship: Alternative Explanations and Predictions'. *The Leadership Quarterly*, vol. 2, no. 2 (Summer): pp. 81-104.

Silins, Halia and Bill Mulford. 2002. 'Leadership and School Results'. In *The Second International Handbook of Educational Leadership and Administration*, edited by K. Leithwood and P. Hallinger, pp. 561-612. Norwell, MA: Kluwer Academic.

Snipes, Jason, Fred Doolittle and Corinne Herlihy. 2002. *Foundations for Success: Case Studies of How Urban School Systems Improve Student Achievement*. Washington, DC: Council of Great City Schools.

Spillane, J.P. and L. Anderson. 2014. 'The Architecture of Anticipation and Novices' Emerging Understandings of the Principal Position: Occupational Sense Making at the Intersection of Individual, Organization and Institution'. *Teachers' College Record* vol. 116, no. 7: pp. 1-42.

Spillane, J.P., R. Halverson and J.B. Diamond. 2004. 'Towards a Theory of Leadership Practice: A Distributed Perspective'. *Journal of Curriculum Studies* vol. 36, no. 1: pp 3-34.

Spillane, James P. 2006. *Distributed Leadership* (1st edn). San Francisco: Jossey-Bass.

Spillane, James P. 2015. 'Getting Beyond Our Fixation with Leaders' Behaviours: Engaging with Leading Practice for Real'. In *Leading Futures: Global Perspectives on Educational Leadership*, edited by Alma Harris and Michelle S. Jones, pp. 200-04. Los Angeles, California; London: SAGE Publications.

Spillane, James P., Megan Hopkins and Tracy M. Sweet. 2015. 'Intra- and Interschool Interactions about

Instruction: Exploring the Conditions for Social Capital Development'. *American Journal of Education* vol. 122, no. 1 (November): pp. 71-110.

Sternberg, Robert. 1985. *Beyond IQ: A Triarchic Theory of Human Intelligence.* Cambridge: Cambridge University Press.

Stoll, Louise and Dean Fink. 1994. 'School Effectiveness and School Improvement: Voices from the Field. *School Effectiveness and School Improvement* vol. 5, no. 2: pp. 149-77.

Taylor, F.W. 1911. *The Principles of Scientific Management.* New York, London: Harper and Brothers.

Thorndike, E. L. 1920. 'Intelligence and its uses'. *Harper's Magazine*, 140: pp. 227-235.

Van de Vliert, Evert. 2006. 'Autocratic Leadership Around the Globe: Do Climate and Wealth Drive Leadership Culture?' *Journal of Cross-Cultural Psychology* vol. 37, no. 1: pp. 42-59.

Vecchio, Robert P., Joseph E. Justin and Craig L. Pearce. 2010. 'Empowering Leadership: An Examination of Mediating Mechanisms within a Hierarchical Structure'. *The Leadership Quarterly* vol. 21, no. 3: pp. 530-42.

Warford, M. 2011. 'The Zone of Proximal Teacher Development'. *Teaching and Teacher Education* vol. 27, no. 2 (February): pp. 252-258.

Waterman Jr., Robert H., Thomas J. Peters and Julien R. Phillips. 1980. 'Structure is Not Organization'. *Business Horizons* vol. 23, no. 3: pp.14-26.

Weber, Max. 1947. *The Theory of Social and Economic Organization.* Trans. by A.M. Henderson and Talcott Parsons. New York: Oxford University Press.

Weinberger, L.A. 2010. 'Emotional Intelligence, Leadership Style, and Perceived Leadership Effectiveness'. *Advances in Developing Human Resources* vol. 11: pp. 747-72.

Woods, Philip A. 2004. 'Democratic Leadership: Drawing Distinctions with Distributed Leadership'. *International Journal of Leadership in Education* vol. 7, no.1 (February): pp. 3-26.

Yang, Yi-Feng and M. Islam. 2012. 'The Influence of Transformational Leadership on Job Satisfaction: The Balanced Scorecard Perspective'. *Journal of Accounting and Organizational Change* vol. 8, no. 3: pp. 386-402.

York-Barr, Jennifer and Karen Duke. 2004. 'What Do We Know About Teacher Leadership? Findings from Two Decades of Scholarship'. *Review of Educational Research* vol. 74, no. 3: pp. 255-316.

Yukl, Gary and Richard Lepsinger. 2004. *Flexible Leadership: Creating Value by Balancing Multiple Challenges and Choices.* San Francisco, CA: Jossey-Bass.

Yukl, Gary. 1999. 'An Evaluation of Conceptual Weaknesses in Transformational and Charismatic Leadership Theories'. *The Leadership Quarterly* vol. 10, no. 2: pp. 285-305.

Yukl, Gary. 2002. *Leadership in Organizations* (5th edn). Upper Saddle River, NJ: Prentice Hall.

Yukl, Gary. 2012. 'Effective Leadership Behavior: What We Know and What Questions Need More Attention'. *Academy of Management Perspectives* vol. 26, no. 4 (November): pp. 66-85.

Zaccaro, S.J. 2002. 'Organizational Leadership and Social Intelligence'. In *Multiple Intelligences and Leadership*, edited by R.E. Riggio, S.E. Murphy and F.J. Pirozzolo, pp. 29-54. New Jersey: Lawrence Erlbaum Associates Publishers.

Zaccaro, S.J., J.A. Gilbert, K.K. Thor and M.D. Mumford. 1991. 'Leadership and Social Intelligence: Linking Social Perspectiveness and Behavioral Flexibility to Leader Effectiveness'. *The Leadership Quarterly*, vol. 2: pp. 317-42.

# Index